Light Up the Dark

Light Up the Dark

An Interactive Memoir

Christine Matics

EMBER PAGES PRESS

Editing and design by Kara Starcher of Mountain Creek Books

ISBN (paperback): 979-8-218-44806-6

This book is for my children,
those who were knit together in my womb.
"For You formed my inward parts;
You covered me in my mother's womb"
Psalm 139:13

Elijah, Tristen, Neya, Harper, & Emerson.
Wherever you are, know that I am with you in the valleys
and at the peak of success, but more importantly,
God is with you and for you.
All things will work together to serve a bigger purpose.

Contents

Part One

*Who Is the Hero? • Deep Sad • I Remember When • One-liner
Don't Let Emotions Drive the Bus • How Are You? • Chameleon
Alone or Lonely? • You Are What You Eat • Prey or Pray? • I Trust You
Put On Your Armor • Teach a Man To Fish • Why Not You?
Quiet Cries • The Stone & The Sling • You Do It • Consumed by Silence
Taste His Goodness • License • You Are the One for the Job
A Table Set For You • Ride or Die • Don't Cheapen Yourself
You are Lord • Royalty • No Invitation Needed • New Garments
Then What? • Whose Voice? • The Lion's Voice • A Roaring Voice
All of the Glory Is Yours • Faith Is Not for the Weak
Can't Leave You at Home • Reflection • Worn • You. You. You.
Naked Truth • Shine On! • Prisoner of the Mind • Industry Standard
Humble Pie • Can You Dig It?*

Part Two

*Where Are My Future Thinkers? • A Grieved Spirit
Grace Is Sufficient • Restoration • The Promise
Barren to Bursting • A New Song • Thought Takes Flight
Looks Like Love • Comfortable with Freedom
More Than You Can Carry*

Part Three

*God Speaks • The Circle of Life • Be Still & Know
The Wild is Chaos & Beauty • Brave Beauty • Starving To Be Full
Kingdom Garden • Rising from Ashes
You Can't Change a Flower • Planted in Good Soil
Still in the Waves • Consider Wildflower • The Rearview
Breaking the Rules • Transcending Thought • Pictures of You
The Giver of Life • Lost and Found • Take Me Higher*

Part Four

*Bitter Roots • Mistaken • Like Arrows • Trust Fall • Preserving Love
Settling In • Hidden by Shame • Bandaids • Master Builder
Hidden Like Treasure • Ask How • Heart Posture
Running on E • Playing*

Part Five

*Tears for Tomorrow • I Forgive You • Let's Get Real • Love Bombing
Just One More • The Princess Wept • Don't You Forget
Numb or Somewhere Between? • Trauma to Triumph • The Blessing
Wasted Rain • Hills and Valleys • Tucked Away • Found In
Mama Bear • Even If • For just a moment • Consider What Is Wild The
Power of Memory • First Love • I Love You, Mommy • By Choice
I Saw That • Settling • Tolerated • Unbelievable • You Are SAFE
Light Up the Dark • Self Sabotage • Yes, Jesus Loves Me
Remember Me • Warring Myself • Shhhh… • The Gift of Peace
Humility or Humiliation? • Guilty Until Proven Innocent
What Would You Say? • You Are Mine!*

Part Six

Thank You

THANK YOU TO ALL THOSE who have supported me by expelling the lies and replacing them with the truth. Thank you to the pastors, friends, and family who stuck by my side in the thick of it. Thank you for bringing water to barren places and speaking to my dry bones, LIVE.

I'd like to honor my sister, Ashley, for her prophetic painting and stunning work painted on the book cover. Thank you.

Thank you, Papa, for stripping me bare and introducing me to parts of You I had yet to meet.

Preface

WHAT HAPPENS WHEN BIBLE STORIES become your reality? When enemies become real and the worst part of your day is not a traffic jam or losing money on a lottery ticket but being stuck in a real wreck and losing what matters most in the world? What about when you see yourself in Job's loss? Or in the false accusations of Jeremiah? Or in David's lack of support? or in Ruth when she was up against impossible circumstances?

When I first considered writing this book some five to six years ago, I was propelled by justice to write it, to expose what had been done. I didn't know what justice meant—to be made right—and I confused it with vengeance. I needed to release my need for God to come wipe my enemies out and replace that need with the truth.

I don't look for vengeance anymore. Those who I deemed my enemies were not. Yes, they did awful things, but I don't hold hate for them. My desire is that they too would be freed from the lie, delivered by truth. Our fight is not with flesh and blood. Jesus died for ALL. He died so that we might walk in perfect union with Him—so that our lives and our hearts would mirror His. Through my writing and my life, I want to point to the One who can do exceedingly and abundantly more than we can ask or think. (Ephesians 3:20–21)

I really didn't plan this book. I knew I'd write it, but it came naturally as the Lord talked to me and I to Him. This is a collection of stories, narratives, and poetry. It is parts of my life laid down for you to encounter and relate to. Some of these poems and narratives date back to 2016. Some offer explanation, and others are just a window into what I believed at the time.

I pray that my story, all the testimonies of God's love, would encourage you to know that you are not alone and that just because things are happening that don't line up with what God says, He has not left you. He never leaves you nor forsakes you. (Hebrews 13:5) I pray that His light would light up the dark places in your life, in your mind, and in your heart. I pray perfect peace would be yours for the taking. Let His light light up the darkness. Let the lies be uprooted by the truth.

If you are like most, with God or not, you may feel defeated. My story is one that felt defeat at tremendous odds with lies as my only identity…but God. I am a living testimony to reflect the heart of God, one of redemption and renaming. A corrupt court system. A move. Another chance. Redemption. This is my story carved out of depression, robbery, and slander exchanged for joy, reunification, and truth. I hope that you find encouragement in these pages to know that God can and will fight for you, and He uses all things to work together for a greater purpose. Nothing is impossible for Him. (Luke 1:37)

Equally as important, I pray this book gives my children who are not in my care—Elijah, Tristen, Neya, and Harper—a look inside my heart. Where the gaps have been filled in by another's illusive understanding, I pray my words and my heart be a reflection of the Lord toward you. I never gave you up. I never walked away. I fought to the bitter end, and I never stop thinking about you, loving you, or praying for you. You were not forgotten. Though life went on to look different, you hold a safe and lasting place in my heart.

The truth will set you free.
John 8:32

Testimony

We tend to pigeon-hole our testimonies as if the biggest stain cleaned or the mistake that could have ruined us should have center stage to show off God's mercy and grace. "That's testimony," we think. Testimony comes from the word *aydooth*, meaning to do with the same power and authority. In western churches we like God to fit in our handbags. That is, if it doesn't fit our agenda or it's too big, we cut Him down to size. In other countries, a natural dependence ensues with the Lord; it's believe or be eaten. It's live it or starve. I don't believe God's desire is for us to hang on the edge of a cliff by a finger. I believe He calls us to stand on top of the mountain with victory showing others how we climbed. Please do not misunderstand me. We all fall short. Our understanding is not His. Our ways look a lot different from His, and surely we have a minor vantage point by comparison to His own, even if we have particular gifts to dream, envision, or see in part.

A testimony contains the word *test* intentionally. A test is taken to obtain a grade or to pass a specific thing. We are never meant to let our tests kill us. They are, however, supposed to crush us. The age-old saying "God doesn't give us more than we can handle" is not only wrong but delusional. Those who stand firm on this saying must have cobwebs on their Bibles.

Every Bible story we look at requires a life laid down. These stories have a testing that could have taken the person out but instead crushed them. God, in that crushing, produces an oil. Oil is part of the anointing. Anointing means "to smear" and was used in ceremonial settings, such as David being anointed king. The image I have is when Simba has the red stuff smeared on his forehead by Rafiki in the film *The Lion King*. This anointing actually happens when he is born. He is lifted up above the rest and anointed as the next king to be brought up to fill the shoes of his father. In the coming years, he goes into isolation, lives a humble life, and rubs elbows with animals whom he could have previously eaten. How is this applicable?

Let us consider a grape. A grape must be crushed to make the wine. Wine is symbolized as new life, a new glory in the Word. Consider the old wine skins and new wine skins. If you put new food in an old container that's not been washed, what happens? The food spoils. It's the same thing. When we talk of new wine, we talk of God doing a "new" thing. He wants to give us new things, the new wine, but we have to be dumped of ourselves and our old ways in order to steward well the "wine" He desires to give us.

Simba was already pre-selected by the king to walk in his footsteps, but he had to go through a crushing process to dump out the old and be replaced with the new. Those lies couldn't remain in his mind, and he had to discover his identity by laying to rest those lies and discovering the truth. We can look at this testing as him running from his purpose because of his uncle's lies or we can see that he considered the cost. With those lies feeling so comfortable, he ran. He ran into the shadows because shame hides. He had fed on the lie that his father's death was all his fault, but even if that were true, it didn't erase who he was and what he was called to. His was a heritage, an inheritance, freely given to become the next king.

Think about Joseph. He was a man who was blessed from the moment he was born and anointed. God already knew his purpose. He was even given a coat of many colors apart from his brothers. All of this honor and treatment could be likened to who he was and what he carried inside, protecting and respecting the gift. He was anointed, favored to carry out a specific task, like a special agent who goes through rigorous training. He was sold into slavery by his own brothers and then the tables eventually turn. His heart posture was mercy as he learned humility and grace along his journey.

If God were to destine you to be on stages around the world for His glory, what would have to happen to ensure the right heart posture? Humility, trusting Him because you've probably got a level of stage fright, and refinement so that you look like your Father. We are born His, but we can begin to look like the world if we don't have His eyes and ears, His heart posture toward things. A gold band is already gold before it hits the flame, but gold only hits the flame to be purified. It's a process to look more like Him. It goes in gold and comes out gold. Refinement is the test. It's the process that takes our anointing favor and crushes us to press every drop.

The testimony is meant to be a story of overcoming. When another reads it, a seed of faith is sown in their mind to bring hope to an otherwise barren land. The mindset changes to "If they could do it, so can I." Women for centuries have birthed children. A first-time mother can become terrified at the thought of birthing for the first time, but other mothers come alongside her to show her the ropes and ease her anxiety. The test is part of the testimony.

Let's dig deeper. "Your testimonies are my heritage." (Psalm 119:111 ESV) Testimony, we know, is to do with the same power and authority. Heritage is one's inheritance. Is inheritance earned? No. It's freely given. We were grafted into God's family by the spilling of Jesus's blood, not for behavior modification but for union with Him. The disciples got the human form that walked and talked with them, but we all get to experience the Father internally, walking with Him always because of the Holy Spirit. If God did it before, He will do it again.

The only time we need to look in the rearview mirror is to transition to a new lane, to something new He is calling us to—a new job, a new leap, a new child. We look back on His goodness to remind ourselves that He has us. When one walks a path, it clears the way for another—that's testimony. They go through the cutting down of limbs, skeeters (mosquitoes), mud, and muck. The sun (Jesus) is always shining on them the whole way. The compass (Holy Spirit) is speaking and directing. We look at the path we have walked to see who got us through, and now others come barreling down that path with ease.

Our testimonies are our lives. A testimony is not a one-time event that could've made us or broke us. Yes, that's part of the story, but it's not the whole of the story. When we start introducing ourselves by that thing, we confuse the testing with the true testimony which is the Lord. I do not identify with what's been done to me or for me, but I am a daughter of the most high King. Ladies, that makes us princesses. Lift your crowns. Hold your head high and know whose you are. Identifying with anything less than the sonship or royal priesthood, heirs that we are, leads us to the gutter.

Do you remember the story of David? God took him from humility to the palace. When David was found to be anointed, he smelled of the sheep (the people). Humility. Think about the movie *Shrek*. A talking donkey sees Shrek's heart while still living in a swamp. Shrek identified as an ogre his whole life, but where does he end up? The palace. Swamp to palace. Ashes to beauty. It's an exchange. How about Aladdin? Street rat to prince. Too many characters, biblical or not, give us examples of ashes to beauty, and it all comes down to identity and humility.

Who do you say you are? So a man thinks, he is. (Proverbs 23:7) Self-fulfilling prophecy. If you believe you are a {fill in the blank}, you'll act like it. If you believe it, act like it. It's a natural occurrence for us to behave from the place we believe of ourselves. If you believe you aren't worth it, you'll sell yourself short in every area. You'll cheapen yourself relationally. You'll undercut yourself for the promotion. What are you speaking about yourself? What do others say of you? Faith comes through hearing. (Romans 10:17) If you hear enough commercials, you'll eventually click "order." They've got you. They sell you the emotions, and you buy in. If you know your worth, how likely are you to buy thousands of dollars in makeup products? Survey says, not likely. Please do not take this as a dis on makeup altogether. A good heart check is testing oneself. When you wash the makeup off at the end of the night, do you like you underneath?

If you don't like you without the thing, it's got to go or be mini-mized. You'll know.

The following pages will detail some of my journey over the years. It's not the whole of my journey but enough to give you a glimpse into my person and to thrust you into my shoes to walk as I did. Isn't that what we do with testimonies? We relate them back to ourselves to connect and take a ride with them. So, let's take this journey together. I'm going to ask that you interact with the pages. Get real. Lay down the mask, the expectations, and the "I've got this" mentality. Allow yourself to digest the material and apply it to your own life. If need be, read it alone. Take your time and unfold your own heart in this reading.

Beginnings

MANY TIMES I WALKED DOWN the aisle of a Christian bookstore or Christian book section opting for something real—something that cut the crap and told the truth. During a desperate time in my life, the churchgoing posture of perfection looked so disgusting to me. I wanted to uncover how they got there.

Be real with me, please. We've all been through hard things, and it's so easy to polish ourselves up on Sunday to act like we've made it. The truth is, none of us have, and our acting like that does nothing for the body nor for ourselves. We need to be real with our-selves to allow God in to do the hard work, and we need others to see our renovations—not just the finished work.

It's hard to believe someone is relatable until they take the mask off and reveal the valleys they also trekked. I promise you that I have a resumé of both valley and mountaintop, desperation and victory. Most don't look like what they've gone through—including myself. I used to become upset whenever I heard "you haven't been through anything" or whichever assumptive line was thrown my way. Now, I thank God I don't look like it. That's the change, my life as a testimony to His goodness, His mercy, and His love.

We are going to dive into the deep stuff and take a look beneath the surface. How else do you heal the surface if you don't know what is lurking beneath?

What is left beneath the surface grows like the roots of a weed producing and choking out the roots of what is stable. Truth must be spoken. It must surface because, without being uprooted, it will continue to spread sickness in the garden. Lies and filling in misunderstandings are what cause division in families, in marriages, and in friendships. When two are joined to one flesh with a lie beneath the surface, a weed grows that burrows its way between the two as they walk away from one another. Being joined together, they pull one another apart by opposition. There is always a bigger picture, and most times truth offers two sides to the same coin. The truth will set you free from the lie.

I didn't know the truth of my conception until my late twenties. The truth delivered me from the bond of a lie because I was told one thing and my mind filled in the rest of the spaces. When we lie to a child, they learn to fill in the blanks. As narrow-minded or innocent as their view is, they learn to impose it must have been self-earned. "Surely, I'm at fault for my parents' divorce." "I shouldn't have been in their way when they..." "Maybe if I would have..."

My knowing the truth set me free because my dad's callous behavior toward me and my mother's emotional avoidance made no sense. I was told I was the product of a party, but the kind of shame that followed me ever since I was a child was whispering suicide. How could that truth be so shameful? Years I should have spent playing sports, laughing, and discovering myself, I spent under a cloak of shame trying to cover myself up. I told myself something was wrong with me. The common denominator. Human experience is to look at patterns of behavior, so why wouldn't I fill in the blanks?

Even when I found God, I wasn't shown the example of how to walk that out nor respected as a child of God, one who actually hears from God herself enough to be guided. We get all hyped up about a child wanting baptism, praying, or accepting the Lord, but no one asks—then what? The ideas whispered from the adversary don't look upon age, stature, or maturity. No, he is ready to pounce on any victim. You are chosen by God, and the adversary wants to take you out.

I thank God for the church camps my mom afforded me to attend, the churches I attended with my dad, and the experiences my grandparents gave me. Those pockets of God were good, but they weren't enough. I didn't know Him as personally as I needed. I had to learn what my faith is actually in. We work out our faith with fear and trembling. (Philippians 2:12) It's not a one-and-done. It's a lifestyle, a life laid down.

I've done my fair share of living double-minded. I watched and learned from those around me. If they don't act like they believe what they are preaching, it's because they don't. As a parent, that looks like "do as I say and not as I do." If it isn't mirrored in and through us, do we really believe it? Those around me set an example and taught me what was safe, healthy, and normal.

My job was to take the things I was born into and conquer them. We are all born into less than ideal conditions, and we must not point the finger of judgment, because we have three more pointing at us. The Bible is clear to judge not lest ye be judged, because the Holy Spirit thrives in unity. Jesus died for all to have perfect unity with the Father—not just the ones we like or agree with.

So while the example I was given wasn't great, I know that my worst day is someone's best day. Someone has always defeated worse, overcome other odds. It's not just you. I've met people with some of the most gruesome stories, and it's humility and grace that keep us moving and keep us grounded.

One of the best things my father did was share his tests and testimonies. I will always respect that in leaps and bounds. With plenty of family and friends reminding him of his past, he didn't hide in lies but remained honest about shortcomings when I was growing up. I believe his telling what he had done and what got him there kept me from trying certain things. I watched others in my family track similar paths, and thankfully, I avoided those. I tracked other trauma-guided paths like theirs but differently. The common thread running through all of us is a test, the odds stacked against us, meant to be conquered and overcome. Let the test press you. Let it shake you. Let it roll you over in your grave because you can't stay there. You have to rise from those ashes to see your beauty in the mirror. We are meant to conquer the things standing in the way of our reflecting our Father.

From a young age, one of the ways I coped was by distancing myself from my household. I never felt like I fit. I felt like a stain, the mistake. Information divulged later only grew that feeling until I realized hearing the truth was actually a wave of relief. I needed to hear that nothing was wrong with me. I remember my mom sobbing and opening up to me and my telling her I thought she didn't love me or want me—that something was wrong with me. She continued wiping te her ars and telling me how precious I was to her, recalling toddler years.

The truth must come out. It must meet the surface. We can't see in the dark without a flashlight. The truth is, if we are not being honest, we look like this un-relatable experience no one has access to. It's great to hear all the successes but hearing someone's failures points to God. We all screw up, and if we are unable to admit that we mess up, how do we pluck the dead stuff and grow? We simply won't, and we stunt our own healing and growth. If we only point to how well we did without showing the struggle, all anyone sees is us. The problem is we are not God. We have cracks in our form, but God is sufficient. We point to Him so that even in our faults, we can point back to what steered the ship back home, what mended the broken. In our weakness, He is made strong. (2 Corinthians 12:9)

The Catalyst

THE MESS PRODUCES THE MESSAGE; the test, the testimony. Let me start with some of the events in their barest form so that you have the backbone of my story. I'd hate to throw you into the following narrative with no understanding, drowning in the words. This entire book is a testament to what I've lived through. When I talk of the test revealing the testimony, I want to ensure I am giving glory to He who is able, not the testing. It is easy to glorify the pain, to live there too long, and to make it welcome in our home like an uninvited guest. I have been guilty of identifying with pain so much that I would introduce myself by it, thinking it would disqualify me from what God had for me. Please read along for context to reference back to, but understand this is not the whole of who I am but rather a glimpse into some of the choices I made and some made for me.

When I was eighteen years old, I chased my childhood best friend to Texas after we got pregnant with our first child. I was too naive to realize what love was or what was required to raise a child up right. I didn't make the best choices, and those choices landed me in some tough shoes. I could blame my ex-husband's family for lying or manipulating the truth, but at the end of the day, I was young and had a lot to learn about what it meant to be a parent and in a stable relationship. The examples I grew up with were horrible at best. (I won't over share those things to protect those whom I have no interest in harming by revealing the truth.)

I lost my oldest son to the state for some time as I and my ex-husband went through parenting classes and counseling. Honestly, we both needed it. We had a lot to unlearn, and a lot more to heal. The healing didn't happen then. Much later, the weeds beneath the surface began to expose their heads. Our oldest son was returned home as we weren't abusive nor negligent, though we had a lot of maturing to do and learned a lot about parenting. What we went through was horrific. I wouldn't recommend ever working with the state, because they are trained to find everything wrong with you, and trust me when I say that all the things you think are normal just cast you as the villain in your own story. It was a learning experience, a humbling one. I'm not saying all they did was right nor that no foul play happened, but I am saying that humility was needed to grow. Accidents were painted with intent, and that is where the enemy loves to do his best work. The enemy takes one truth and runs with it like he has a license to slander and unfold your whole life. Every parent is imperfect no matter how hard we try.

We went on to have three more children, and eventually after the third, we moved back to Ohio to be nearer to family for support. That was a hard move because my church family in Texas was my family. I loved worshipping, and though I didn't realize the anointing I was carrying and pouring out, I was also earning God's love. However, that earning is not love; we can't earn what is freely given.

While in Ohio, pain grew like the roots of a weed beneath the surface. It sought to choke out any life we had as a family. Boy, did I love my kids! My friends used to call me Super Mom. My only identity was being a mom, and I shut God out. Earning and striving didn't afford me what I yearned for, so all that pain I had as a child took a back seat because I had kids to think of. I had pride in who I was as a mother, but I left my husband to suffer in the corner alone. He was silently suffering from PTSD, replaying war in his mind while I was busy planning birthday parties and dancing with the kids in the kitchen.

The truth always comes out, especially out of the mouth. For me to fill in the blanks of what I didn't understand about my husband was so easy. His pulling away emotionally was due to a deep pain I couldn't understand, and while I should have been there, I was too busy making other plans. Yes, I was young. Yes, I had kids back to back, and by the age of twenty-three, I was a mother to four. But no excuse in the world can combat how self-serving I was. Sure, I made meals and told my husband how much I loved him, but I had no foundation. Our foundations swept us both into relationship and responsibility at young ages, both carrying weighted traumas that we naturally tucked into suitcases to survive and provide.

We can only give what we have. Where earning and striving exist, we are only as good as our behavior. We are only as good as what brings us to the table. We become God because we don't need Him nor do we care what He has to say about the matter. Talking to God and truly having an intimate relationship with Him seemed like another chore to pile on to being "Super Mom," wife, caretaker, and student. No thanks, sign me up to do it alone, and that's exactly what I did. I learned from a young age to thrive under pressure. I like pressure. I want to be pushed. I want a challenge. I don't feel the same now at thirty years old. The weight is too much to bear when we unpack those suitcases and realize the truth of our upbringing, what happened, and who we actually identify with.

My relationship with my husband had issues. He had behaviors manifesting from the pain and seeking comfort in things beyond me, and my tongue was slanderous. I've always known my mouthpiece was my best asset. I knew the connection between writing, speaking, and song was my tongue. However, when we have something not submitted to God, it's submitted to something else. I can't outright dismiss that I had a relationship with God, but it wasn't a true relationship. It was forced. I still grew in discernment, but what I used my tongue for was not good. I cut down my husband when the blanks I didn't understand grew. Whether he was doing something or not, I filled in the blanks with assumptions and decided who he was by what he did. Isn't that what we do—so many of us who grew up in the church? Sometimes it's better to avoid the religious example and be dumped of self later in life to only be filled back up. Growing up in church taught me to perform and earn God's love. How do you earn a free gift? You don't. It's like running on a treadmill and looking at the freedom in front of you—always out of reach. God's love is found inside in rest and stillness, in surrender. (Let me be clear—my experience with God was not all bad up to this point. I chose to see just the pain.)

I don't want to glorify pain here, so I will spare you the details of what my husband or I did, but we needed healing, desperately. We looked good on the outside. We both grew up with enough trauma to tell us how to bury it and move on. Everything is a seed, so burying trauma creates roots, and sometimes we water the pain instead of the promise. We had our ups and downs, but that trauma we both had felt like the suitcases taking over our entire closet. We needed to unpack them, but what time and energy do you have when you have responsibilities?

Humility is the key to freedom. Writing these battles on paper feels scary. Barring my heart and mind to whomever picks up this book is terrifying, but is it really? Through all of this testing, I've learned that man fills in the blanks where understanding fails, but God is truth. He sees. He knows. He approves of me, and that is freedom.

If anyone could use a slice of humble pie, it's me. The purpose of a memoir is honesty and vulnerability. It's looking at the raw self, flaws included. In a world of likes, comments, opinions, scrolling, and numbing, it is easy to become prey to neglecting real work. If, on the outside, we look good, I don't mean necessarily physically, but if we look the part and can say "we are fine" without actually thinking about it, how far removed are we from humility? Humility to me is to be meek in understanding how BIG God is in comparison to how small we are. It's not feeling lowly or pathetic but rather understanding that in our weakness He is made strong. "My grace is sufficient for you, for my strength is made perfect in weakness" (2 Corinthians 12:9) We know that in our weakness He is made strong, at least we have the Scripture memorized, but do we read on? "...Therefore, most gladly I will rather boast in my infirmities, that the power of Christ may rest upon me."

How many of us will boast in our weakness so that we give God the glory in His redemptive power, grace, and righteousness in us? Not I. Often, I'd rather just avoid revealing what God has brought me out of because shame is an ugly robber. Satan loves to steal our voice. If he can keep us balled up in chains of shame, we won't ever speak. Our tongues can produce life, people! As long as we live wrapped up in shame and reliving and recounting what our accuser has spoken over us rather than humbly noting what God has done in our weakness, we remain silent. There is power in our worship and praise to God. "Now when they began to sing and to praise, the LORD set ambushes against the people of Ammon, Moab, and Mount Seir, who had come against Judah; and they were defeated." (2 Chronicles 20:22) This army's praises fueled a fight against their enemies. God gives each of us gifts as an authority over the enemy who doesn't actually have power. He can whisper a lie, and our job is to either replace it with the truth or run with it.

We all give God praise! Declaring with our mouths that He is above all else. "Death and life are in the power of the tongue, and those who love it will eat its fruit." (Proverbs 18:21) So then, what fruits are we eating? It brings to thought the Scripture about how a man thinks of himself. "For as he thinks in his heart, so is he..." (Proverbs 23:7) Be humble in your shortcomings and God's grace in your life will also affect the way you internalize who you are. Concealing your weakness is like a boulder you refuse to give to God who is much stronger than you. No matter how strong you think you are, your legs will eventually give out. Let's give over to the Scripture, "...God resists the proud, but gives grace to the humble." (James 4:6)

The Test

WHILE I CONTINUED TUCKING MY trauma into the suitcases in the closet, our family life moved forward. To celebrate our second oldest's birthday, my husband and I took our four kids to a local event called Canal Days to ride rides. What started out as a fun day turned into terrifying. While on a moving ride, our oldest son unbuckled himself. He was tossed to and fro, hanging on by one arm. His father and I were busy looking at our youngest in her stroller and didn't see the drama unfolding with our son.

A woman to our far right witnessed what was happening and began shouting. Suddenly, the ride director stopped the machine and went to our son. She was hysterical, thinking it had been her fault. It wasn't. Our son was banged up, but he only had scrapes. He was looked over by an EMT, and we were given a ride incident report. We ended up leaving the event because we didn't want any other accidents. Our son seemed fine other than all our kids being upset we had to leave.

Fast forward two weeks, give or take, and we had to deal with an incident where one of our kiddos peed in a container and on kids' reclining seats while staying with my mom. My husband and I were away on an anniversary trip when this took place, so we weren't sure of exactly what happened. Looking after four little kids plus my young sister could be a lot, and the gated playroom was around the corner from the bathroom and kitchen. Who knows what and how it happened. It doesn't matter now. However, this event set the ball rolling.

My kids unanimously decided my oldest had peed in the playroom. I was so worried we would have an issue on our hands as he went into school since publicly peeing on things was frowned upon. Did it matter as much as my fear took over? No, it didn't, but I still retained the experience of CPS in Texas in my memories. I never allowed myself to heal from what happened there. Yes, we learned, but I had a lot of pain still rooted in those memories—chewing on lies of being a horrible mother for accidents that were painted to be more, abandonment from those who should have been there, and accusations from my own mind deciding that I'd never be good enough. After all, if I would have pulled him further away from the hair straightener, he would have never grabbed it. If I would have used my brain and didn't make some of the errors I did as a first-time mother...But those "ifs" were me believing I was only as good as my behavior. That sort of thinking always leaves us defeated because we believe we will make the wrong choice.

As parents, we will have accidents. I cannot tell you how many things I've seen over the years that by definition of the state of Ohio would leave parents without their kids. That's awful. Being a parent these days has no grace. It is perfect or failure, and too many mothers battle this inside their minds. Pinterest mom, check. Keeping everything tight and pretty, check. Ensuring God is in your life enough, check. The Disney song "Surface Pressure" was the perfect theme song for most of my life—until I lost everything. Pressure will eventually cause you to break.

Back to my oldest, my ex-husband and I decided to spank our son as he would not fess up to peeing in the playroom. Honestly, I was concerned with being judged and what would happen if he did it at school. No, it wasn't about image. It was about a looming fear of not being enough, and that fear would look me in the whites of my eyes soon enough. I needed to identify with someone other than my pain.

When my husband went to spank him, he pulled while our son pulled away. We heard a pop, and suddenly my husband was taking him to the hospital. Later, an orthopedic surgeon saw calcification on an x-ray and revealed that the arm was previously broken—that day on the ride at Canal Days. We are talking about an oblique break, usually associated with sports injuries because of how severe the break is. Even after the break was pulled on and revealed, my son never asked for Tylenol—nothing. I imagine he has a high pain tolerance, because so do I. (I have now birthed five children.)

After the hospital visit, a case worker became involved, and we had an impending court case on our hands. Looking at the break and seeing prior involvement with child services four years prior painted a pretty obvious explanation I'm sure. But, they were wrong. A case was opened, and all our children were removed from our home. We attended parenting classes and jumped through every hoop, yet we were never afforded a single visit. Our kids were home one day and gone the next. Familial association is a right afforded by the Constitution. It "protects the fundamental right to intimate association, which includes the familial association between parents and children," according to the American Bar Association. We were not given a single visit with our children to see how we interacted with them, nor were our family members. My mother told me that when she called in to see if she could visit with my children, our worker told her that she would not see them again.

We worked toward "reunification," yet every blank was filled in by assumptions. The assumptions were run with and afforded the state the "right" to take our children even though no one else was hurt and we had proven the reason for cause in our oldest son later. Our judge refused our orthopedic surgeon's x-ray proving calcification and not abuse. No photos, letters, or facts were considered—at least none that didn't prove their goal.

Facts didn't matter. A criminal case was opened toward my husband even though my son had no bruises or anything making this sort of break possible other than the ride incident. He was found innocent. It didn't matter.

Every single thing in our lives was flipped upside down and made out to be wrong. I walked on egg shells without a correct response. I was backed into corners to admission or remission. Accusation, boy, is it a fun ride. Our court case was the most traumatic thing I had ever experienced. The great thing is that once we've been dumped of everything, we can only be filled back up. And I was dumped of everything.

During the case, CPS found things they didn't like or filled in with their own understanding, such as my ex-husband and how he managed PTSD. Rather than acknowledge his involvement in the military, his service was belittled and scoffed at. He needed help and so did I. Years later, I would also be medicated for PTSD after everything that happened during this case. Imagine being an ant under a magnifying glass, and no matter which way you move, you are burned by the sun. That is what it often looks like to be involved with family court. Facts don't matter. Opinions reign. Group think in a small town becomes like a god. You get a few folks who think they know you, and it's like bitties in a beauty shop who control your future and your children's futures with their tongues. Is there accountability for slander and libel? No. None.

But God.

I'd like to take a moment and acknowledge that for years I hated these people for what they did and said. I hated the lying and slander. I hated them for the things they were never held accountable for and then I realized I had to forgive.

It was killing me to identify with pain, to hold on to what was done not only to me but more so my kids. Do you know the pain of not knowing your child's new name, where they are, who they've become, and whether they are protected? I know that pain, and I wouldn't cast it on my worst enemy. I had to learn that my enemies were not people. I do not wrestle against flesh and blood. I've always been a mother, and often we will find our call in the midst of the thing we fear most. Even before I had children, I was the oldest to something like twelve or thirteen other siblings. I don't know how many. I was naturally selected as their leader and had to be prepared to have the answers and to nurture them, whether in the school yard or at home. Ironically, children are drawn to me everywhere I go, yet motherhood is where I've experienced the most loss.

Back to the story, or rather the testing. We ended up losing all our children to the state, and we could do nothing about it. The state didn't see us as fit parents. We could have gotten help, but the story they decided on dictated our future and our children's—or so they thought. You see, God gets the final say. No matter what accusation Satan throws at us, he already lost. The testing is only to produce a testimony.

Near the end of our court case, we got pregnant with our youngest son and we got a divorce. Getting pregnant again seemed like a tragedy in itself, thinking we'd lose him too, but it was the biggest blessing we could have hoped for—the beauty in the ashes. One of our lawyers encouraged us to move to another state and advised that this was a "witch hunt, like nothing they'd seen before." We took the advice and moved to Washington nearer my ex-husband's family.

After the move, I was in a place where I didn't know a single soul and nearly a country away from my family and friends. I had lost everything, my children, my home, my husband and best friend, all of it gone. My ex didn't move right away as he was still finishing up college classes. I got a job in Portland, Oregon—just over the border—and I tried to maintain my sanity and not let the fear win every day of the pregnancy. Eventually, my ex joined me, and we tried to rekindle our marriage, but there was no mending all we had gone through. It destroyed the very feeble foundation we built our relationship on from the beginning.

After we birthed our son, the state of Ohio issued some sort of alert to the hospital. Case workers and doctors found their way into our room. One doctor looked at me, looked at the paperwork, and said he didn't believe anything written on the page. Interestingly, I have no idea what was written down. He looked at me with my son and said that he could easily observe the great love I had for him. He said that even if everything they said was true, I should have at least had visits with my kids. He asked me if I had visits with my kids, and I confirmed that I hadn't.

When the workers came in, I was so terrified. Truth didn't matter, so what would stop them from taking my newborn boy right then and there? I looked at my ex-husband and told him I couldn't do it anymore. I had every intention and imagination of jumping from that hospital building and leaving the world behind. I just needed to wait until the nurses changed shifts. I felt nothing. I was so hollowed out that, without any hope inside me, I felt like God was dead. How could He let me go through this? How could He let my oldest be medicated, isolated, lied to? How could He separate all of my children? WHY?!?

But there was no reply.

Pain was my closest confidant, the only thing I trusted, because pain was the only thing that remained steady and reliable.

Getting Real

A CASE WAS OPENED IN Washington to uncover the truth, and contrary to the allegations, we were given visits right away. We participated in parenting classes that taught us how to see ourselves as parents again. It filled up the barren places with hope.

For the first time, we started getting real help. My ex received help for his PTSD and was being seen for probably the first time, and as was I—seen for the first time, truly. My counselor introduced EMDR and walked me through healing as a parent and as a child. I had developed PTSD, feeling replaced as a wife and as a mother. It felt like the common thread was me. Something was wrong with me. I was told several times that I didn't need to learn anything as a parent but that I needed to love myself. I hated myself. "If only I would have..." I recalled those voices of shame and blame louder than any hope could ever offer.

But now, I had hope. We worked all the hoops and had regular visits, and those visits turned into overnights, then weekends, and then we had our son back fully. Today, we share our son between our homes. We never reconciled our marriage. My ex-husband moved on, and I'm waiting for the man God brings my way. I've had enough of trying to find the right one myself, and being married again is not my end goal. I had to learn my end goal is God. I've learned to seek first His kingdom though some days my lens is not as selfless.

I can't unfold every detail of everything that happened. It would take a long time. I have re-written the telling of this test too many times to count, and each time there is so much more to tell of pain, of triumph, of inhumanity and injustice, and of joy and miracles. In the following pages, I try to uncover much of that as I bare everything to you, my reader. It doesn't matter whether you believe me or not—whether you see one side of the coin or the other. I share my story as context so that the lens is understood—at least somewhat. Without some grasp of what happened, it would make the words, poetry, and narrative that follows indigestible.

I'd love to sit here and tell you that everything afterward was conquering victory after victory, but walking our faith out is done with fear and trembling. Nothing is easy or weak about being a follower of Christ. I've fallen more times than I'd care to admit.

After the court case in Ohio and while in Washington, I used men to fill the void of intimacy I craved but couldn't put my walls down enough to let in. Call it a relationship or a one-night stand, it all points to the same desperate need, doesn't it? I yearned to feel something, but I didn't want to face what was going on. I hated myself and saw every lie as gospel. When I looked in the mirror, I saw someone worth using and told myself that sleeping with my ex from time to time was reconciling. While it is understandable that I could not easily cut the tie with a man I'd loved since I was about thirteen, I was not reconciling as much as I was allowing myself to be used. And I used men to find intimacy, a fleeting satisfaction, rather than allow what I truly desired—a space for intimacy with God. For the sake of honesty, my vices have been men, Netflix, social media, and vanity, anything to take my eyes off God.

In my pursuit of intimacy, I downloaded a dating app and ended up dating someone for a few months. While I was happy at first and he was and is a good man, I just distracted myself from what I needed, Jesus. Society tells women to get back out there when something doesn't work out, and I'm not saying dating is wrong. For me, I needed to be vulnerable and trust God. In all things, we should yield ourselves to what God is trying to do in us. He knows what is best for us and protects us from what will bring us pain.

I chose pain over living most days until the last two years when I started to realize I was identifying with pain and not who made me. Replaying lies and slander on repeat in our minds, not taking thoughts captive to what God says, and staying in memories will only cause us to reproduce pain. I needed to dig up the weeded lies and replace them with truth—rooted in who God says I am above everything else. He is my authority. He decides.

Sin consciousness will only produce more sin. What we look at, we will move toward. Ever heard the saying "Show me your friends and I'll show you your future?" Faith comes through hearing. We begin to look like who we spend time with. When learning to drive, you'll find that if you are not looking ahead and instead looking at the semis, you'll start to move toward them.

Being conscious of who God is and who you are will naturally cause fruit to come from that place. What we believe will birth fruit. A plant goes through a lifetime of pruning dead stuff off to produce. We are the righteousness of our Father. What is being pruned is the lie (the weed) at its source (the root).

I give God the glory for loving me through my flaws and the distorted identity I had that produced such fruit and behavior. He was and is always there with open arms ready to wash me clean without seeing a blemish. Now that the veil has been lifted and I see my identity for what it is, those same behaviors are not permitted in my life. I don't have to try and behave. The fruit of the spirit is naturally birthed from the tending of good soil and knowing who He is and, by extension, who I am.

I'm learning to be more obedient day by day. Faith comes through hearing. Even if it isn't someone else we lend our ear to and we can tune out the broken record of family, friends, and others, ignoring their accusatory words, sometimes our worst enemy is ourselves. Mine was. Mine is. I listened to accusations so much in my mind that I allowed myself to become angry and bitter and to sink into a pit of despair for too long. However, I will always get back up because I know God made me for such a time as this. I will speak. I will write. I will sing. I will do what He asks of me.

For my children Neya and Harper, you are bright lights to this world. Your song and your beauty are gifts, and I'm so grateful to have birthed such incredible people as you. I'm grateful that I am afforded to see you as I do, and I hope that we only grow in relationship and in intimacy. I'm so proud of who you are. It has nothing to do with what you do or say, but I am proud of who God made.

For Emerson, I love you deeply and infinitely, and now that I know grace and love, I am so glad to freely give it to you. I'm sorry for the way that trauma took the show when it did. I'm grateful that, at your tender age of four, I can show you the mama God made in all His glory. You were the gift that saved my life. Yes, God saved my life, but He used you to do it. You used to be the reminder of everything I lost, but now I take pride and joy in every single smile and in every moment I get with you.

Elijah and Tristen, I'm sorry that I have not yet been afforded a chance to know you. Your sisters found me through a miracle, a prophetic word come to pass, but you, I have longed to reconcile with and know you ever since I last said goodbye. I never stopped thinking of you. I never stopped praying. I never stopped hoping and believing. I love you all dearly and I'm sure to be one proud mama at who you each are—whether I know you or not, because if God made you, and He did, you are a treasure. You are each a treasure worth knowing, finding, discovering.

My story isn't over, and neither is yours. The following pages will give you an insight into some of the refining I went through in my lowest times in the valley and on the peak of the mountain. I could share so many testimonies of God's faithfulness, and I hope that I've touched on enough in this book. Those who know me personally hear testimonies of God's love, favor, and grace in my life regularly. I want to give Him glory, for He is good no matter what is done to us or for us or what we do. His love is lasting, and it's not dependent on behavior modification but real heart change. Surrender opens us up to His wild love for us.

Would you do me a favor and take a page from my book? Bare your heart as well. Be honest when prompted to ask yourself questions. My hope is that you find healing and connection.

Let's get real together.

PART ONE

IDENTIFY WITH HIM

"I'm no longer accepting the things I cannot change.
I'm changing the things I cannot accept."
— Angela Davis

Who Is the Hero?

THE HEROES IN MY SMALL-TOWN America, as small-minded as they come, were those enforcing, policing, or dictating in some form. They were high up on the food chain looking down at the bad guys, the addicts, the broken. The reality was, it was pride versus the broken. Those in power weren't stronger, better, or otherwise the antithesis of those deemed bad. They just chose to assert themselves, their views, and their power, usually derived through money, over those who had no power. They were celebrated as having it together, strong, capable, and untouchable, especially to those feeling the wrath of those decisions with no checks and balances.

The antiheroes were the other side of the binary, those who were poor and perceived as powerless. The community I grew up in is about fifteen to twenty minutes from other neighboring communities, and the fog settling on the hearts and minds of the residents was not determined by republican or democrat, liberal or conservative. Rather, the fog was determined by whether there was an openness to vulnerability or a brick wall of judgment and control. Understanding, cultural diversity, or education was not the prelude to humility. It was not the solvent.

Whenever I return home, an eerie chill sweeps over me knowing that the town has continued to solidify a binary between powerful and powerless or what may be perceived by some as rich and poor. I can't quite simplify it to money. I'd like to simplify it to one's true state of heart, whether they have genuine good or not. I can't categorize by religion because for some religion is a cover up but, for others, it is the drive to be their absolute best. Relationship with the Father is the difference because we are all flawed and our default mode implores us to sin, to hate, to war. God causes a change in our hearts if we allow not just because of a title, but because of a surrender.

This response was to the question: Who are the heroes and who are the antiheroes in your community? In your family?

Re-reading my response to this black-and-white question in college begs more attention. God looks at the heart of a person to determine its surrender. A person is not defined by their behavior but by who made them. No matter how much your child upsets you at a given time because of a temporary behavior, your love for them is sturdy and lasting. It doesn't change. God's love supersedes ours.

It's incalculable how much God changes our hearts and minds. I don't like to look at pruning as a season but as a lifestyle. I want to look more and more like the Father as I go through this life. Our identity is in Him regardless of behaviors or beliefs. You cannot simply decide your blood is not of your mother and father on earth just as you can deny God all you like but He made you in His image. The pruning happens as you naturally spend more time in His presence. We look like what we spend time with.

I nearly threw this excerpt out, but I think it's important to show the growth in understanding. I didn't wake up one day and understand all. God grows me as I spend more time with His Son. Just as with a flower, it must be watered and sit under the sun's gaze to flourish. And so must we.

Deep Sad

I FEEL THIS DEBILITATING LEVEL of sad lately. It's not just missing people but lacking any connection. I've had so much taken from me that it is often hard to want to roll out of bed. I thought that it would be difficult not having Emerson for the summer, but part of me was excited to explore and go on adventures in a new place. I was so wrong. I hated his being gone and the silence in the night. I missed tucking him in and reading him stories, him asking to cuddle, and our movie nights. It brings me back to the sorrow of losing every memory with my kids.

I hate the way I feel and I spend every second I have awake digging trenches to bury the pain because I can't face any of it. I can't do normal things like keep a photo album full of memories for visitors to flip through. I can only imagine how God must feel thinking of our breaking hearts. I saw photos of my son Tristen recently, and I've been a wreck ever since. Seeing how lifeless he looked made me feel so much rage and pain, just completely helpless to add any joy or counter the thoughts of pain he might bear.

As I get older, I have no other explanation but to call my experiences heavy. I can't carry them anymore. I feel myself breaking beneath the weight of all the pain, the shame, the heartache, the trauma. I feel like I could collapse at the thought of plastering on a smile to show the world I came back stronger. My mind feels exhausted from being so damn restless and I'm tired of running from what is home, from anything that seems real. I find myself escaping so that I don't have to sit with my thoughts. I always admired that I didn't slip into addiction with what I've made it through, but I have unhealthy outlets all the same. If I drink, I drink to escape so I don't do it often for fear of living my genes. If I smoke, I escape into a painless lull to numb the noise. When I go anywhere I crank the music because it deafens the thoughts warring in my mind. I'm tired of the noise replaying how I'm not enough no matter how hard I try. I often feel like a failure with voices of inadequacy playing so often you'd think we were friends.

This is what it looked like to find solace in the arms of my feelings. What was familiar came a warm hug and the thought of healing those wounds was terrifying until it wasn't. Encountering this word is so encouraging seeing how far I've come in no longer making shame my friend and overwhelming emotions my home. My home is wherever because the Lord is my home.

I Remember When

I REMEMBER WHEN THE RELEASE was enough to get me by.
Sure, there is getting drunk or high,
but I mean a long night binge of a reality that's not mine—

online shopping and dropping a dime.
But nothing fills this void.
I've found pleasure in men who don't know my name.
An empty glass and "I want you" slur felt the same
as a temporary fill for a deepening hunger.
Quick love won't fix it—can't fill it no longer.
Yeah, I know Jesus. He found me there,
but He isn't a wizard, and those pains have deep tears.
Some things I couldn't say out loud for I'd be silenced if I did—
no fault in a man when I was just a kid!
Same story on repeat. The enemy hungers to eat,
finding fuel in our innocence.
Slithering into our minds for a little entertainment,
he loves to plant lies.
Do you know what it is to near the age of thirty,
still fighting to scream at night and always feeling dirty?!?
Have you felt a cold grip on your lips as you tried to scream out
with nothing to say while you remained in a drought?
For most years, I have felt the weight of silence,
breaking bread with my fears, getting cozy with anguish.
A lifetime of feeling trapped under this steal door
leaves me panicked and breathless always wanting more.
What can I say except this elephant has followed me,
made himself a home on my chest, and I want to be free.
But as a believer, it's more reason to stay quiet.
Because if you had Jesus, wouldn't He help you fight this?
He would if He could, but I've held this pain close.
It's even closer than Him, and it's clouded what I know.
Jesus is a gentleman, and He would never force His way.
He wants all of you.
With trauma as your comforter, it's easier to stray.
I remember when moments of breath felt like I was weightless,
a change from this mess.
I want to look back and remember
a time when full surrender was given and freedom was mine—

the start of a journey, parting ways with my pain,
and with nothing but goodness and joy to gain!

One-liner

"HI MY NAME IS CHRISTINE, and I have five kids."

Okay, so my conversations don't start like that, but like a tiresome cliché, I've begun to roll this line in my mind like an anxious teenager practicing in front of a floor-length mirror. How and when do I introduce this truth that has become a noose around my neck?

To the mothers I meet, I either know so much about parenting for being a one-child mama or the assumption of having one child traps me under ignorance and lack of experience. To a prospective man, I stare at the wall of misconception that stands in the way of understanding.

How do I come out from this blanket of shame? I might as well start my conversations with "Hi, my name is Christine, and while I seem bubbly and often have the most energy to give, I am cloaked in an identity of shame. I guess that's my real name. Let me start over. Hi, my name is Shame. I don't ever sleep, and I always tire. I bask in pain."

Chalk it up to lost identity or whatever you'd like to deduce, but I've felt trapped for so long that it seems easier to avoid introduction and just slip away into isolation. There, I don't have to tirelessly rehearse a speech, plaster on a smile, or play pretend for even one second. With that said, let me take you into my mind without introduction and simply as a journey to understand a lens I never recommend living—the reason I have just one of five children.

I'd strongly recommend a sermon titled "The Delusions of Shame" by Legacy Church in New Philadelphia, Ohio. This message began to pull me from the miry muck of shame. Shame causes you to hide. It guides your hand to identify with the pain you've grown to know and love. It's a familiar friend.

I invited shame in at a young age, feeling nearly consistently that something was wrong with me. I couldn't watch the news without viscerally feeling what the people endured. I tucked myself behind closed doors and mourned the pain another felt. I'd have a dream that came to pass weeks later and chalk it up to a very detailed déjà vu.

I learned to conceal anything that was not largely accepted. I grew up watching Turner Classic Movies. I adored the films that valued family, love, and conquering. I wanted to escape the world I lived in. Too many called me an "old soul," but I knew it was more than that. I felt like I was born in the wrong decade.

In school and at family functions, I was mocked for being too dressy—surely, it must be a cry for attention. While I was suffering and desiring to be known by God, the dressing had nothing to do with earning love. I adored ruffles and curls, hoop skirts, and cinched waists. I found a great fascination in the femininity of old. In high school a few girls repetitively told me I looked like a Brat doll or Barbie, trying too hard, mocking my identity. I left and thought I'd find more acceptance at the rival school. Day one, worse. I was asked what class I was teaching several times while walking the halls, and then the rumors began.

Having your identity, style, and zeal mocked sucks. Truth be told, looking back at this girl, I had a thing or two to learn. It should not have bothered me so much what anyone had to say because what God says matters. When you find accusations knocking at your door and you answer the door in defense, it only keeps coming. I had to learn that God is my defender and only His words matter. Truly, we can mock or push away what we don't understand. One of these things doesn't look like the other, but that doesn't mean it's wrong. This is what starts war. We fill in the blanks of what we don't understand. What we fear becomes something we hate. How can we despise what we don't even know? I didn't know all the reasons that others mocked, but what I've known to be true is that the reasoning doesn't matter so much as standing in who I am unwavering.

Shame. It's not a friend as much as a familiar comfort in isolation and hiding. If shame is hiding, then the way to come out of hiding is confidence. Knowing who you are no matter what anyone else says or does, remaining stable in knowing it, and exuding it is confidence. I could give you hundreds of examples of the way shame cloaked the joy in my life, but I'll leave these ones here.

What is your one-liner?

_____

_____

_____

_____

Can you identify shame in your life?

_____

_____

_____

_____

What do you think it reveals about your heart posture
and things that need changed?

_____

_____

_____

_____

Don't Let Emotions Drive the Bus

EMOTIONS ARE FROM GOD, BUT we are called to steward them well. They are not to blind us, govern us, or stunt us.

Don't excuse yourself because of your "personality." That is really an excuse to sit in the dirty diaper you were born into. We were all born into chaos, into drama, into pain and shame, into lies. Don't stay there in what seems comfortable.

Be comfortable with freedom. Stay there. Grow and then follow the Lord to the next place.

I've heard a lot of stories in thirty years. Some are the more soul-crushing stories of aging out of the foster system abused and neglected, molested by parents, ridiculed to the point of a gun to the head, accusations almost taking someone out.

Don't believe the lie that you are alone or the only one. Instead realize that one who becomes a great leader, one with poise and power, doesn't draw from their own painful well. They draw from a healing well that never runs dry. They understand the concept of leaving the old garments for the new.

Who are you? Whose are you? Those two questions matter. Believe different so that you do different.

Stop with the one-liners of "this is what you get," "it's how many families do it," "it's what happens medically." Last I checked, my God made the doctor, the lawyer, the judge, and everyone else with a heartbeat. He knows best. If you didn't hear it from Him, throw it out. Allow Him to love on you and to heal the broken parts so that when you receive love, your cup can hold onto it, falling on good soil. If your container is broken, like old wine skins, it will release the new wine and tarnish it. If you cannot let go of the pain you are holding, you can't hold the blessing nor can you know how to properly steward it. (Luke 5:37–38)

Be honest with yourself and seek God with all your heart. Get desperate for Him. You've tried all the money, women, drugs, alcohol, everything. Did it fill your Christ-sized void?

Cry out in contrite heart and watch what God will do in and through you. He wants your heart, and everything flows from your heart—the issues of life, that is. (Proverbs 4:23)

What has your heart?

_____

_____

_____

_____

One way to sort that out is to ask this question: where do you spend all your time, money, and energy?

How Are You?

WHEN I'M ASKED "HOW ARE you," I usually offer a half-truth. I'm not the person to say "great" when I'm not, and my face could tell a thousand words before the lie broke my lips. If someone asked today, they'd get a lie. I'd say, "I'm fine, and how are you?" Anything to change the subject, because the truth is, I'm not okay. I'm torn by my thoughts and my feelings. I'm not okay that my life has been anything but ordinary. I am alone in my suffering with no group or chat to join where others collaborate in their suffering and success. I am not okay with being torn apart mentally and emotionally as I contemplate the ways I can and will let my daughters down. I am trapped here, against my will, with my only better judgment being my son. He has kept my head above water.

I asked my girls if they'd like to see their brother and me for the holiday. They both gave a resounding no. Why? They wanted a visit sooner. My oldest said boldly, "I want you to come to my birthday." She repeated herself with the statement, "You'll come for my birthday." Those words were uttered from her lips many times with the certainty that she would get what she wanted. Between her statement and her heart's desire as plain as her eyes and my younger daughter holding my hand and pulling close to my side, they're mine again. I built a barricade between myself and their love as I shuddered at the thought that I'd never be their mother. But those moments broke every lie that stood in the gap and left me undone. My heart was full of so much joy, it felt as though it would burst at the seams.

But then, I came home to my reality, and I could do nothing to be their mama, to love them deeper, to reach further, to show up and be there. I've all but erased my desire to feel after spending my first week slumped in a kind of hopeless depression.

So supermarket guy with your sideways smile, brand new kicks, life just beginning, I am not okay.

Reading this entry from two or three years ago, I remember the pain, but it's foreign. I still have days that hurt, but I know that even reality doesn't dictate truth all the time. God gave me those children; He entrusted me and knew them and me before He knit us in wombs. If He knew all this would happen and it isn't good, then He isn't done. When I see my daughters, they beg for more time with me. Their spirit is drawn to mine. I've always said that animals and children can discern a heart quicker than most adults. I know that God is good and He works all things together. He makes everything beautiful in His timing, so why should I worry? Why should I cultivate a heart that barricades the very love bursting through? I won't let any pain define who I am. I won't let another man take my joy. I won't give away my peace. I protect what is mine. I hold dear to the truth of what God says and who He says I am—not as a hope but as knowing full well who I am. Do you hear what I hear? Do you see what I see? A child knows.

———————————

Chameleon

I THINK IT'S TIME TO retire the chameleon. I don't want to look like you. I don't want to give up my colors to blend into your gray—to trade my joy for the mundane. I used to think blending in with the crowd was a gift, but now I understand that standing out is harder than it looks. These days you all look the same—painted faces, hair extensions—no name. Eyelashes that fell into your soup or becoming someone I'm not as I've been duped.

I want to look back on this place and feel good about the woman I was and the chances I took. I want to show my boy what it's like to be more than an object, a toy. I'm not some throwaway, depreciating, losing value. I'm timeless because I know my worth. It's not determined by fads or by your words. So that lizard won't get my glory. I'm taking a stand and retelling my story. Blending in is for the weak. It takes strength to stand apart.

Alone Or Lonely?

WHY DO I HIDE INSIDE myself and present a woman that's not me?
Why does shame act like a prison holding me hostage?
Set me free.
Love is like, I know it's call,
but I'd rather take sex instead of intimacy.
Many men have known my body,
but which of them have known me?
Sin begins to invite me in,
and I feel comfort in my bones.
At this point in my life,
I'll do anything to avoid being alone.
But what is lonely anyway?
A place inside myself.
I can be in a crowded room
and still feel like a doll on a shelf.
An image speaks a thousand words
or so they like to say.
Who is this *they*,

and don't they know that image will soon fade away?
Alone, inside myself, I sit;
this life, I beg, I want to quit.
I don't have the strength inside of me,
I want to love and be loved for me.

When you are hungry and you don't want to take the time for a home-cooked meal, you run by a drive-through or throw something in the microwave. Culture looks like this. While cell phones and socials have their place in the kingdom, connecting people around the world, they also entice a quick bite to eat.

Growing impatient and wanting a quick fix, we have developed a slew of dating apps to shop for men and build-a-Barbie of our own. We've got one hand on a man with the heart we want, another with a guitar, and the others bolstering the word "Christian," so we are hoping it's more of a lifestyle than a mirage. If we are honest, does this searching and striving really reflect knowing that God has a man or woman for us? Or are we, in our desperation, trying to fit a puzzle piece in our puzzle, often cutting it down to fit our own agenda? Listen, I know folks have met through dating apps so let's not throw the baby out with the bath water, but when you are wrestling with your identity in Christ and hungry for love, often you'll settle. Think about it—why don't we go grocery shopping when we are hungry? We end up with popcorn, cookies, and a candy bar for the way back to the car.

The root (lie) driving my weeds (behaviors) was that I was alone. I felt that God had abandoned me, but an even deeper root connected to things in my childhood and marriage was tucked away. I was hungry to be known, and because I wouldn't go to God, I went to the substitute. You can eat greasy cheeseburgers and fries all your life, but eventually, it will wreak havoc on your body. This is what it looks like to use sex in place of intimacy—to fill a Christ-sized void with a counterfeit. It's not the person who is counterfeit. It's replacing what you need with what you impulsively want. The flesh wars against the spirit, but boy can I tell you how much easier the way of escape is when those thoughts come having been planted in the love of Christ. When you know who you are and whose you are, the substitute is no longer desirable. Your new eyes show you exactly what is going on. It's like looking at a cub when everyone else sees a lion. You just don't see it. Rather, you do see it and no one else does.

Don't sell yourself for a cheap glass of wine and small talk you'll regret in the morning. Your hunger reveals a void that needs filled. Don't avoid the void. Instead, fill your tank with the good stuff so that you don't burn out and look for another gas station five miles down the road.

"For He satisfies the longing soul, and fills the hungry soul with goodness." (Psalm 107:9)

You Are What You Eat

HAVE YOU NOTICED THE CONNECTION between mind, body, and spirit in your life? Do you notice a pattern among what you eat, what you do, what you listen to, and what comes from it? Do you notice when you are intentional about what you consume and release a shift happens? It's as if your body comes into agreement with what God is doing. That's not irony. A connection exists because the body is the temple of God.

Maybe this is why fasting is so important—releasing what we deem as necessary and replacing it with the Word to sustain and to grow closer in a time when our flesh is crying out. Fasting is a help for temptation. We cut out the things we have been told we need to survive. For a length of time, we dump out ourselves and what our flesh desires so we can be filled up to overflowing by the Lord. Fasting might look like giving up Netflix binging, smoking, or drinking coffee. It can also look like giving up food and drink for a set amount of time. When the thought arises to consume the things you declared not to, go to God's Word. When you get angry, go to God's Word. When you get tired, go to God's Word. When anything rises in your flesh, submit it to your spirit by going to God. God says it subdues our flesh to the Spirit. No longer does the flesh have the say in leading us to daily coffee runs or chain-smoking, the desires of the flesh.

We house much more than organs. We house what matters beyond a Netflix binge, what to wear to an upcoming event, the opinions of others, or a bad grade. We house what changes the world. The gravity of that reality brings clarity to any confusion. If we could imagine housing the Lord in our bodies and knowing we are the doorway He uses, His hands and feet here on earth, wouldn't we want to both look and behave like Him but also be healthy and capable?

We have authority over many things, but we also have a flesh to subject to spirit. We can do that by putting good things in and getting good things out. Often I'll notice a check engine light—that's what I call it—when I become low and in my head. If that happens, I not only need to remind myself of what God says and take inventory of what I'm inputting but also ask myself what I am releasing. Personally, I release by going to the gym or through writing.

We can slip into fight or flight when our thoughts are not taken captive, circling back to old wounds and traumas. Before you know it, the walls go back up and we react out of flesh, not how God would look or sound. Through meditation or getting out of our headspace and causing our flesh to submit to the Spirit, whether by working out, listening to praise music or life-giving words, or meditating and being still to know, we can cause our bodies to come back into agreement. By agreement, I mean into agreement with what the Lord says about something for ourselves. If we are feeling low, chances are we are running on empty, and honey, it's time to pull over. We all know we can't give from an empty cup, but we also know we shouldn't keep driving just because we've got a full tank. Rest is important. No one gets anything done depriving themselves of rest.

Be careful little eyes and little ears. Put good in and get good out. Discipline your body and mind to agree with the things of God. We don't always want to go to the gym, but when we finish, we feel amazing and capable. We don't always want to eat healthy foods, but when we don't see the terrible side effects and burn out that follow eating poorly, we feel good. We don't always want to hear from God, but we listen anyway. We get still anyway. Still your body, your mind, your spirit. Be still and know.

Prey or Pray?

I HAVE THESE THOUGHTS THAT I'm the worst example
of what it means to be a Christian.
I play them on repeat,
and they act just like a melody singing me to sleep.
Awake to all the pain inside—avoiding the news as it lies.
Whisper kindly in my ear, all I want is to disappear.
Your name is hope and brings me to life.
My flesh is at war, holds me hostage in this fight.
My inner child wants to be seen, wanted, loved,
know what it means
To be held and cherished and loved the way
She needed love and chases each day.
I know You want me, Your call beckons me,
but it hurts too much, can't You see?
I'm not enough, I'll never be.
I'm a slave to my sin and it follows me.
Hunts me down like weakened prey,
I'm tired of running. I want to stay...
In a place to call home like the one You have for me.
Where sin is a lie and I have victory.
It hurts to be real on this battlefield.

I Trust You

TRUST IS A FUNNY THING, isn't it? I can't think of a better image to encompass trust than to imagine falling into the arms of a perfect stranger or maybe even someone we know without any reservation in our muscles—just release. So what about falling into the arms of something invisible? Ah, well, that is faith which may well be the same thing concerning God. Taking that leap of faith into the unknown is to hope that something good is on the other side. Sometimes that looks like following the voice we know to the other side no matter how crooked the trees and dark the shadows in our valleys. Trust requires being blind to what is in front of us as we take the hand of one who sees far greater, deeper, and wider than our limited human view. It is this leading and following that relates back to the sheep.

Sheep behave in odd ways so it's only rational that biblically we would be compared to sheep. Go search what it looks like for a shepherd to round up the one lost sheep that keeps going back to the same pit, desperate to its own nature, only to be rescued and repeat the cycle. Without the shepherd's lead, the sheep's life looks like insanity, trying the same thing over again but expecting different results. Dare I say, it is sheepish. Leaning on the understanding of one who has a multi-dimensional view (the shepherd) rather than a one-directional view (the sheep) is wise, considering that God's ways are not our own. His thoughts are not our thoughts. If He said it, don't boast in your own temporal emotions or current station, but trust His Word that He sees more and knows more than you do.

God is God, and we are not. Pride is so foolish—foolish enough to cast ourselves as the main star in the film of life because surely we see all and know the intentions and hearts of everyone around us. It seems irrational when reading these words on the page, but leaning on our own understanding is an easy accomplishment. It is allowing our emotions to dictate our day, mulling over the words someone else said or what we decided, playing them on repeat, and investing in things that oppose the kingdom of God. (Who doesn't love a good Netflix binge? I'm there, when and where? I'll bring the popcorn.) God's plan can require us to put aside distractions that take our attention while we focus on what He has asked of us.

Doing the hard part is to lay our life down daily to what He asks of us; it's sort of the gig. We did sign up for this. If we want to look like Jesus in our lives and attain the kingdom promises, we must submit in order to reflect the heart of God. Trusting Him with our time, money, and energy reflects what matters in our lives. I once heard it said that whatever we spend our time, money, and energy on is our god. That's heavy. Think about it. What do you seek when you are sad? Stressed? Anxious? Afraid? How about after a long day?

I'll go first. Sometimes I shop to distract from pain. I've crammed in long Netflix binges to avoid obedience or healing. Who doesn't love the idea of living vicariously and never having to put their own heart out there again? What about the stash? Food? Alcohol? Pornography? You name it, there is an "addiction" for it. I hate that term. It bears so much weight for something that has been deemed to have a hold on someone. Lock them up, throw away the key, and slide meds under the door. An addiction is something that takes the place of God. It becomes a crutch to escape this life and its pain and suffering.

Trust looks like going to God as your first source. (I'd love to say your only source, but it's important to have friends, family, and church.) When you are hurting, go to God. He is the Great Comforter. He gives better advice and intimacy than anyone else. When you are angry, tell God. Contrary to societal standards, it is okay to feel angry, and it's even more okay to tell God. Why would you conceal what He already knows? Do you think He has thin skin? That's not the God I serve. He created the heavens and the Earth, breathed life into the fabric of existence, knew us before we were conceived in our mother's womb, spread blankets of royal oceans, and created every scale, color, and species to its own.

That God, He wants all of you. He doesn't want just the part of you that says all the right things and shakes their head in agreement, pleasing all who pass. He wants the breaking, the hurting, the anguish, and the disappointment. Let Him have it. Know who you are talking to, but give it to Him. He can carry the load, I promise. Trust Him with your whole heart, the tied-up-with-a-Christmas-bow, bitter, irritated, disappointed, silly, childlike, easily excited, complex person you are. He doesn't disappoint as His Word does not return void. It is exceedingly and abundantly good and true.

When you were little, do you recall a parent or adult telling you that when you have kids you'll understand? It's not necessarily about experiencing the exact same thing as being given a new set of eyes and increasing understanding as you grow. God is good. He is for you. His love is not a tease. In time, truth unfolds as it always does, and we can make sense of what was once a blur. What are you waiting for? Let go. He will catch you!

Are there areas of your life you struggle to trust God with? Ask Him why. Ask Him how you can trust.

_____

_____

_____

_____

_____

_____

_____

_____

_____

Put on Your Armor

ARMOR IS NECESSARY. IT'S OUR protection. "Therefore take up the whole armor of God, that you be able to withstand in the evil day, and having done all, to stand." (Ephesians 6:13)

Put on the armor of God. How do you do that? Let's break down Ephesians 6 into bite-size pieces. Grab your Bible, read verses 14–20, and then follow the commentary for each piece of armor.

"Girded waist with truth"—Armed; fastened garments with

a belt keep clothing on lest humiliation befall you. The opposing thing to truth is a lie. Keeping your garments of truth close ensures you don't fall prey to a lie.

"Breastplate of righteousness"—A breastplate protects the heart. The heart is contended as deceitful in the Word. Unless you know not to be led by emotions and tossed by the waves, you'll find yourself drowning often. Righteousness protects the heart and means to be conformed to God's own being, just. The more time you spend with someone, the more you begin to look and act like them. You no longer desire the things of the heart, foolish things.

"Shod feet with the preparation of the gospel of peace"—To shod is to bind under foot and notates footwear. Wearing footwear protects and prepares you to go. When you take hold of peace, let it soak into the hidden depths of who you are, and you will mirror it wherever you go.

"Above all, the shield of faith to quench all fiery darts of the wicked one"—A shield protects against darts, against destruction, and against pain. Faith is to believe and put trust in. The opposing force for faith is a lie, unbelief. To be assured in things hoped for and not yet seen, standing firm looks like reminding your mind what God says, not watering the weeds in your garden but rather pulling them at the root and tending to other things. To pull something from the root, we must ask ourselves, who said it? If God didn't say it, toss it. That weed has got to go. When standing behind a shield in the armed forces ready for battle, a warrior stands firm ready to meet the enemy, protected. Stand firm on the truth, on what you know to be true. The Lord is not a man that He should lie nor does His Word return void. Don't waver in that, regardless of what happened in the past or what reality looks like; if He said it, believe it.

"Helmet of salvation, prayer and supplication, watchful with perseverance and supplication"–A helmet covers the head, the mind, which is really where the battle is considering it was already won. Prayer is to bind or vow. We are coming into agreement with what His Word says over our lives and those around us. That's the battle—taking every thought captive to the obedience of Christ. The example Jesus gave us when temptation came to Him is: Does it represent what God says? No. What does He say? To bind reminds of a contract, a covenant made to us from God back to Abraham and binding to all creation along with the blood shed for all. Salvation is to be safe or rescued. When you know you are safe and rescued, you rest in a grateful state of mind, grateful for what God says, not your own will or another's words. Once safe, you trust that the one who saved you is good and will not cause you harm.

"Speak boldly"—I've heard it said that when you know a thing, it is easier to teach it. I had someone recommend that I teach a concept to another while learning to fully grasp what it was I learned. The Bible calls this studying yourself approved. "Be diligent to present yourself approved to God, a worker who does not need to be ashamed, rightly dividing the word of truth." (2 Timothy 2:15) The more you know a thing, the more you can speak boldly on it. We waver when we don't understand. If we don't understand or recall a recipe, what do we do? We look at the recipe and read it again. When we don't hear what someone said, we ask them to repeat it. Church is not meant for us to simply consume and go home, mindlessly returning each week. This is a participation in the kingdom of God. You want peace? Your pastor isn't going to hand that to you. You must seek the Lord. "And you will seek Me and find Me, when you search Me with all your heart." (Jeremiah 29:13) He knows His creation well enough to know when you are playing and when you are serious.

In other countries, believing unto the Lord is life or death. They know themselves to be safe. In America, we have so many choices that we often become unsteady looking at all the other options with less of a shelf life, things that are fleeting and momentary. Yes, go do that and see how you feel the next day. Go ahead, jump into bed with that person, and then when they stop talking to you, find someone else. When you conceive, you'll feel differently. Hindsight.

The Word gives us wisdom to see through a different lens. We can't look through the lens of the world and think we will be on steady ground. Being bold for the truth takes spending time with God. You cannot know someone through another person's encounter. Don't rely on your mama's prayers for you. You are grown. Stand up, dust yourself off, and walk. As a child, we need lots of love and direction, and our parents are gentle with us. It's not to say as we age that goes away, but more truth is given. "Therefore submit to God. Resist the devil and he will flee from you. Draw near to God and He will draw near to you. Cleanse your hands, you sinners; and purify your hearts, you double-minded." (James 4:7–8)

If you want to be trusted with much, you must be trusted with little. To much is given much is expected. "...For everyone to whom much is given, from him much will be required; and to whom much has been committed, of him they will ask the more." (Luke 12:48) As we mature in the Lord, He gives us more. Our heart changes, and as we receive, we can be trusted to steward well the gifts we are given. A good heart check with finances, for example, is "if you had a million dollars, what would you do?" If your answer is self-seeking, that should be a check engine light.

We need to know ourselves, to know our check engine lights, so that we can refill. When you want to know how a machine works, what do you do? You read the manual. Same thing here. God created us. He knows His creation, and no one else knows the inner workings of this machine beyond the Maker. Dig into the Word. Sit and write; digest it. When we eat a meal, we chew and swallow. We are made full. Are you hungry? Starving for truth? You must sit down (be still and know), come to the table hungry (seek Him with all your heart), and meditate on the Word. Read. Ask questions. Dig. Someone who wants to know another will pursue relentlessly. They will ask questions and spend time with them. Adore their words.

"Ask, and it will be given to you; seek, and you will find; knock, and it will be opened to you." (Matthew 7:7)

Can you locate the chink in your armor, your weak spot? How can you use the words in Ephesians to be better prepared in full armor?

_____

_____

_____

Teach a Man To Fish

DON'T HANDLE IT FOR THEM. Teach them how. Teach a man how to fish rather than fishing for him. The gift of showing someone how to do something is far greater than doing it for them. In one situation, you are discipling, and in the other, playing God. See, if you are doing it all for them and giving them all the answers, they flunk the test when it comes time to apply what they've learned. You must take your hands off. Show them how; don't tell them. Be the example, not the solution. Jesus is the only solution, and being anything but an example puts all eyes on you rather than pointing to who taught you.

Aren't you still learning from the teacher? Yes. If you are a good student, you are still humble enough to listen to the teacher and find that you still don't have it figured out, regardless of how it looks to everyone else. Keep knocking. Keep asking. Keep being dumped out and filled up again. Pride comes before the fall. Lean on His understanding, and in all your ways, acknowledge Him, and He will direct your path. It's not your way or the highway. It's His way or the ditch. If you want to take the wheel, He will give it to you and be right there to love, comfort, and teach you in the ditch. He won't mock you, but He will teach you and allow you to learn from your own choices—leaning on your own way.

"Trust in the Lord with all your heart, and lean not on your own understanding; in all your ways acknowledge Him, and He will direct your paths." (Proverbs 3:5–6)

When you don't know how to do something, ask. When learning how to operate a piece of equipment, you go to the manual to inquire from the maker. They know how their machine works. As much as people can be helpful, they see in part. They will never fully know or see your heart as God does. They see what is permitted for them to see—to pray and stand on truth on behalf of that person but never to behave as if they know the whole of the person. God knows the heart of His creation. Ask Him. He knows.

No one likes a know-it-all. It's good to study yourself approved, but without humility, it's not relatable and ineffective in the kingdom of God. If you "have it all together" all the time, no one relates to you because your mask is on so tight that you don't even look human. Untouchable. Be vulnerable and true. No one is God. No one has all the answers even with as much as God may show or reveal to you.

When playing games with a friend, I always catch myself muttering to the cocky opponent, "You know what comes after pride, right?" I answer my own rhetorical question with "the fall." Humility is desperately needed, especially in the US, since the message we hear from the moment we learn to lift our heads is "You got this!" Truth is, you don't. God's got this. He has you, and that is why you are here, why you are favored, why people are drawn to you. They honor you because they honor the Father. He who accepts me accepts the Father. (Matthew 10:40) Rejection works in much the same way, but understand that "we wrestle not against flesh and blood, but against principalities, against powers." (Ephesians 6:12) What is inside your "enemy" doesn't like what you carry. The Holy Spirit works in unity. When one carries the Spirit of God, the other vessel recognizes it. Recognize. You feel me?

Don't take things personally. It has nothing to do with you. The flesh wars against the efforts of the spirit. (Galatians 5:17) Do you want to know if you heard it from God or your flesh? Is your flesh arguing with you internally? "Why would God ask that hard thing of me?" That question is uncomfortable, and it's likely God. He asks us to do the hard thing. The principles of the kingdom are not those of this world. It's like the earth is flipped on its head. He who loves his life will lose it and He who loses it will find it. (John 12:25)

So then, don't do it for them. Teach them how and who. You yourself remain teachable, moldable as with clay.

Why Not You?

THERE WAS NOTHING SPECTACULAR ABOUT any of the disciples or the most-watched TV preacher out there for God to have chosen them. Nothing was holy about them. Their humility allowed the Lord to work in and through them. Everything but the kingdom of God is fleeting, so they weren't qualified for the job before the obedience. He qualifies the called. He does not call the qualified. God has a long history of using the misfits, rejects, and society's last choice. He uses the least of these.

Who said it? Whose words haunt you and cast a shadow on your dreams? Words are powerful. Consider this: words created the universe. God spoke, and the words brought life. Words come from our tongue, compared to the rudder on a ship, and are said to be sharp like a sword as with the Word of God. A rudder is a nautical control used to direct the way of the sailor. Linguistics matter. The power of life and death is in the tongue, so speaking on things that are riddled with gossip, fear, or anger will lead us down a broad, avoidable path.

But faith, it comes through hearing. Whatever we listen to repetitively, we birth faith to. When watching a commercial or considering the intentional algorithm of a social media platform, pay attention to the things that stand out. Soon enough, you're clicking "order." Whether it be a repeated image or words, we are both impacted and do the impacting. Who said it? Whose words have superseded God's in your mind?

Often we speak about transforming our minds, and I've found little actionable advice to do so. Look at your environment. Take inventory of who and what you surround yourself with. What kind of music do you let represent the soundtrack to your life? That's ultimately what it is, a soundtrack to reflect the inner workings of your life. We spend ample time replaying our favorite songs. What are the lyrics to your favorite song? Make sure it lines up with your character or one you seek to have. I'm sure you've heard the saying "show me your friends and I'll show you your future." Now consider the movies you go to. Think about what goes into the making of a film. Music, clothing, intention, behaviors—all are intentional choices. I'm not asking that you over-analyze a film or a song. I ask that you allow the Lord to convict you so that you don't mimic the wrong things played out on the screen or playing in your earbuds. So, who said it? If God didn't say it, it shouldn't bear weight to your identity.

Does it align with God's Word and with His character? I pray you have ears to hear and wisdom to discern the difference between His voice and any others.

Quiet Cries

I AM AT A LOSS for words when there are so many to say and memories have flooded my mind and broke the bank.

I wish I could find the motivation because I know I need to speak for you who have no voice, you who have been slandered, your joy stolen, not by choice. You children displaced by corruption in place of gossip, not part of a beauty shop, but festering beneath a system made to steal justice.

Justice stolen is not just, not for us,
those who cower at the enemy's plan to divide and conquer.
But who's conquered? Not I. Not anymore.
I still need you, Lord.
You are the ache in my heart,
the burning under my feet to go,
send me, not I.
A battle not yet defined.
Speak, a word spoken.
They know not what they do.
No correction, not from You.
Action. Faith without works is dead.
You said, I need to move.
Help me come unglued.
It will shake loose the barriers built around my broken heart,
the pieces I hide from all,
the places where I feel small.
Help me move in You!

For without You, I do not do.
I do not know.
I am not who You called me to be.
I'll take a knee
and bow in a world that preaches ME, ME, ME
aiding injustice in its reach.
Teach me, O Lord, to take a knee
in honor to Thee to lead my every step,
You who give me each and every breath.
Jehovah Jireh, my provider, give me wisdom to speak
and humility when I am weak.
Fill my cup when I'm undone
and don't leave me thirsting when I run.
Pull me down from pride,
reveal my heart when I try to hide.
Break chains my forefathers bore;
help me to know my strength in you, Lord.
Let my words be few;
let them reflect only You.

The Stone & The Sling

THE STONE IS YOUR VOICE, your weapon. Wield it well. Sing with
reverence! Speak with intention. Write with authority. David, don't
worry about the giant, no matter how the situation looks. What we
perceive as a mountain is a molehill to His vantage point. He created
all things. His Word divides the wheat and the tares. Rise up. Take
your place in His body. Speak. Write. Sing. Your portion is victory
and rest. There is no war to win. He won it! Rest and obey.

You Do It

"Is ANYONE AMONG YOU SICK? Let him call for the elders of the church, and let them pray over him, anointing him with oil in the name of the Lord. And the prayer of the faith will save the sick, and the Lord will raise him up. And if he has committed sins, he will be forgiven." (1 Peter 5:13–20)

In the Old Testament, *elders* refers to the older, wiser generation that held the church authority; however, according to John Piper, founder and teacher of desiringgod.org, "It is worth noting in passing that the office of priest, so prominent in the Old Testament, is not taken over by the early church. Prophets and elders (Ezekiel 7:26) have their counterparts in the church and these titles are used. But there is no official counterpart to the priest, for, as the New Testament teaches, the whole church is a 'holy priesthood' (1 Peter 2:5) or a 'royal priesthood.' (1 Peter 2:9) We who are in Christ have all 'been made priests to his God.' (Revelation 1:6) Each individual has access to the holy of holies, God's throne of grace, because of the once-for-all atoning death of Christ. No officer in the church has the function of mediating between the believer and God."

Having no need to meditate and having direct access, any of us who have the "prayer of faith" will save the sick. This is also why taking inventory of the company we keep is important. I'm not saying that you should weed out all your friends, but allow the Lord to do some natural pruning. Sometimes the pruning happens with your person, and other times He will remove people from your inner circle. There are seasons for everything under the sun. When needing a great deal of faith for a thing, it is good to have friends who have the faith to stand by you, behind you, and all around you in prayer. Having Doubting Thomas in this season could be difficult as faith comes through hearing. What we lend an ear to matters.

"So then faith comes by hearing, and hearing by the word of God." (Romans 10:17)

Consumed by Silence

SILENCE CAN CONSUME US, BUT there is power in lifting our voice to the one who is able! In your "can't," He CAN. He is the "I am" to your able.

"Now to Him who is able to do exceedingly abundantly above all that we ask or think, according to the power that works in us, to Him be glory in the church by Christ Jesus to all generations, forever and ever. Amen." (Ephesians 3:20–21)

Our flesh is insatiable in its hunger, and it will consume all its lusts without a submission to authority greater than itself. Are you tired of being distracted by the pretty things? Do you want substance lasting? Would you rather a feast or a fast-food meal? Distraction is the enemy of original thought, made to war with an illusive reality. The sounds of chains rattling can be found in the cry of desperation.

We give so much toil to things that don't deserve a tear. He wants our ALL. We mourn the loss of relationships, staring at the bottom of a carton of ice cream wondering why they chose someone else. Who gave them the authority to hurt us like that? Who gave that drug the power over us? Who told the lies that they had the power to curse our name? We did. Cry out to the one who is ABLE! He made you. He knows you.

People are often consumed by experience that affects their lens, so how can you expect them to give what they do not have? We put this Christlike pressure on people expecting them to fulfill us when only God can. We must be dumped of everything that doesn't look like Him so we can be filled up.

Silence is not your portion. You have a voice. You have a song. You have language. Your tongue is a sword and so is the Word of God. Use them. In Ephesians, we learn about our weapons to fight this invisible battle that has already been won. Well, that seems counterproductive, right? What are we fighting? We are coming into agreement with the truth. The battle is only in our minds. Jesus paid the price for all and we must come into agreement with such a reality. We consume the truth so that the lie goes running. When you consume an antibiotic, it fights off the sickness, right? The sickness in the Garden of Eden was caused by a lie. What flows from our lips represents what we have been stewing on. We are what we eat. Are you picking up what I'm putting down? Eat the word; reproduce it.

"And take the helmet of salvation (knowing you are saved by the blood of the Lamb—protects the mind) and the sword of the Spirit (the Word of God defeating the lie), which is the word of God; praying always with all prayer and supplication in the Spirit, being watchful to this end with all perseverance and supplication for all he saints (many sticks are difficult to break)—and for me, that utterance may be given to me, that I may open my mouth boldly to make known the mystery of the gospel, for which I am an ambassador in chains; that in it I may speak boldly, as I ought to speak." (Ephesians 6:17–20)

Regardless of the chains offered by the situation, your emotions, or what happened, declare the Word of God as authority because "now faith is the substance of things hoped for, the evidence of things not seen." (Hebrews 11:1) An ambassador is someone who represents a thing. What does another experience when they experience you? I'm not saying to put stake in what one says over God, but a pattern may be revealed in what they see. The trends they experience and the patterns take them to God. They reveal a deeper thing needing addressing and healing. Let our minds not be offended. Truth is offensive, but truth sets us free. Let's be willing to correct our path so that we don't end up in a ditch.

Don't be silent. Speak the Word of God when nothing is left to say. Speak. Sing. Lift up a hallelujah even here.

Taste His Goodness

JIREH, COME AND EAT FROM my table.
Sometimes it gets hard to swallow the truth,
so I cut it down into bite-size pieces I can chew.

I often find the taste to be bitter so I refuse,
push the plate away because what's the use.
My father tells me it's good,
but I refuse to taste because it isn't something I know—
how could it be though?
I've spent years eating manna, the Israelites' "favorite" dish,
convincing myself it wasn't a large enough pool of fish.
Sure I guess I'll give it a try,
but that wasn't the full truth.
It was sort of a lie.
I could control how much I could take
by spraying ketchup all over the place.
After I took a bite or two
I found that this flavor was brand new.
My taste buds danced,
and I couldn't take a breath between bites.
This meal prepared for me was more than meets the eye.
Its flavor was plenty and its story stole the show
with morsels that left me filled and my heart all aglow.

License

GOD GIVES US LICENSE TO have authority over our body. We have free choice, choice to decide and to do, to set our minds and carry through. When love is uncovered, because it was there all along, it's of free will. We have the right to choose or deny Him. Love is not control, and it's not forced. He doesn't want slaves. He wants a relationship. When we decide to do things through our own flesh, we wind up paving our own path of destruction through pain that begets hardship for ourselves and others. Our minds are hardwired to debate, retaliate, destroy, tear down, and defend. When we surrender our hearts and our minds and seek a relationship with God, our minds and hearts begin to seek new desires, His desires. As those things change, it's like our paths become one, and our heart's cry lines up with His future and His destiny for us.

Our thoughts have power. We can tell our body to jump, climb, sit down, stand, go, and stay still. If we have the ability to command our bodies like this in our own flesh, imagine what it would be like if we surrendered to the will of our Father? When our thoughts are lined up with His and our hearts open, God has a direct channel to us to not only speak to us about what He would like to do and say for us and through us but more importantly the connection can't be severed. We reunite with our Creator. Like a child that has been gone for some time, the restoration brings with it nuances that look like the Father inside of you.

You Are the One for the Job

NESTLED IN BED WITH LIPS pressed on your shoulders and toes in my hands, I am back in the hospital room the day you were born, tinier toes gently tucked between my fingers as I feared losing my new gift. I hadn't imagined that you'd be here next to me, cuddling each night and morning, kisses and hugs, never enough. Closer and closer now my heart allows. You are mine.

Did you know that blood cries? When Cain killed his brother, Abel, there his blood cried on the ground. (Genesis 4:10) How about the Lord shedding tears for us? In the story of Lazarus, Jesus wept. (John 11:35) We are made to govern what we see by what we know. The truth will set you free. If God gave it to you, don't you think He knows what He is doing? If He is Alpha and Omega, beginning and end, He is well-aware having "...chose us in Him before the foundation of the world, that we should be holy and without blame before Him in love, having predestined us to adoption as sons by Jesus Christ to Himself, according to the good pleasure of His will, to the praise of the glory of His grace, by which He made us accepted in the Beloved." (Ephesians 1:4–6)

His selection of us for the job has nothing to do with behavior modification but rather our knowing who we are in Christ. Looking in the mirror of the Bible, we will either see Him looking back at us or shame. Do we know who we are and whose we are? The goal is that Christ is like a mirror to us that we might reflect His love and grace, His countenance. We were made in His image, right? God doesn't make mistakes. He already knew the choices we'd make long before we became the mother or father. Why do you think God gave Himself to the foolishness of man to be killed and resurrected? This is a crazy kind of love to defeat the grave.

You are the woman for the job and the man for the job. You are His so you have His power flowing through your veins just like your child(ren) also bears the same blood. No one can replace a Christ-sized void just as no mother or father can replace your being a parent to your kiddo. Your child is half of your blood as we are also grafted into adoption with the Lord by His blood. We are made in His image, and they are made in yours and His. Hell hath no fury like the love of our Father. Our love for our babies only compares. His love is relentless. He is faithful to complete every good work He starts. (Philippians 1:6)

A Table Set for You

EXCUSING MYSELF FROM THE TABLE I was told to set and prepare, one I once felt pride in putting together, I shift my eyes from the things He has designed for me. What is it that seems to rob the celebration set before me?

"Set the table. They are coming," You said. "I am making a table in the presence of your enemies."

Yet, this resistance exists as a force field to keep me from the very things promised. The promised land was avoided for forty years while the Israelites wandered in the wilderness. Obedience looks like a step of faith—a step against all odds negating the deafening sounds of fear. I have a seat at this table.

No matter what it looks like in your life, God works in "impossible situations" to bear the fruit of your faithfulness in obedience, to your birthright. It is not our portion to pour from an empty cup, but we must know the well to draw from.

Without a state of overflow, any water given leaves us in deficit. Like a lamp that cannot shine without being plugged into an outlet, the intention is to be plugged into the source. The electricity is the Holy Spirit and being plugged in allows for a constant stream of light not affected by the darkness.

Think on the verse in 2 Chronicles 7:14—"If my people who are called by My name will humble themselves, and pray and seek my face, and turn from their wicked ways, then I will hear from heaven, and will forgive their sin and heal their land."

We want what is rightfully ours, and there is a step involved in faith—obedience. It's our step to meet Him at His Word, to act in agreement with—"faith without works is dead." This is not meant to induce striving but aligning with the kingdom at hand. Seek first the kingdom of God and all else be added to you. (Matthew 6:33)

Humility sets us in rank under God's authority. Praying and seeking His face naturally rewires our brains and hearts to desire what He desires. What we speak and what we listen to direct our paths. When we put Him first, those fleshly desires soon fall away as He gives us a new heart and mind renewed. In Romans 12, the passage reminds us to "present ourselves a living sacrifice" and implores us to "be transformed by the renewing of our mind…" (Romans 12:1–2)

As with a bouquet of wildflowers, each has its own purpose, its own beauty, and its own function in the environment it resides in. Together, in difference, a bouquet is made complete. It is much the same with the body of Christ and with the written Word. We each differ in function and beauty but reflect God's intention and heart.

The table has already been set. Will you taste and see that He is good? Will you believe that you belong?

Ride or Die

THEY TRYIN' TO KNOCK ME down again. Tryin' to take me out. But I know Your worth, and all that's within me cries out, "My God, where are you now?"

You're always near me. You've always got me, even when I've fallen away. I couldn't do a thing or say a word that would take Your place. You're my ride or die, go all night. You've got me like the waves. It's wild and unknown, but it's You I crave.

They tryin' to knock me down again. Tryin' to take me out. I hear their whispers in the night—they get so loud. But I'll remind myself where my help comes from. You're my everything. I don't walk alone!

So whatever it takes my heart cries. Whatever it takes; keep my spirit alive. You are the possible truth in odds up against a wall. You've made every impossible thing look small.

You are the God of possibility—the God who lets me rise and fall. You teach me which path to choose and you're with me when I lose it all. I don't have to worry—every provision has been made, and it's peace that I have because it is everything that You gave.

God is consistent when we are not. When God says a thing, He is going to do it. His Word does not return void, and He is faithful to complete every work He starts. We can rest assured that what He says will come to pass. We only have to believe.

When you are the sort of person, like me, who gets frustrated when you don't get back what you gave, things get a little muddled. We ask ourselves questions like "why is this person treating me like this? I didn't treat them like that." I have to remind myself, "They are not you, Christine." We even expect God to act like we do. Is He going to flake out like we do? Abandon like they did?

We give love and grace freely not expecting it back. We are called to love the Judas in our life. It's easy to love the Jesus. It tests what our faith is in. Sometimes we expect God to move as we move just like we expect a person to do as we do. He is consistent when we are not. That's good news. We do not fill in the blanks with our understanding, our timeline, or the way we would do it, because God is not us. He is a man of His Word. We may change, but He never does.

Call on Him to be your ride or die.

Don't Cheapen Yourself

WOMEN ARE NOT PRODUCTS TO be put on and stored on a shelf when not in use. Pull another down—that's got the juice. Put me on for a show, shine me up—what a glow. That's enough sass out of you. Keep on talking—I'll come unglued. Sit there. Look pretty and don't dare make a peep. Calm down and do not weep. You're meant to be seen and not heard, wanted but not kept. But today's woman cries for a real man.

Rise up, men of valor, we need your victory. This world has eaten your humility. Rise up. Rise up, Dad, and take your place. It's our children who seek your face. We've been forced to stretch far beyond what we were made for. Our feet simply won't fit in your shoes. This won't do. Rise up! God is calling after you.

Men are needed. Period. We need fathers to rise up. We need husbands to take a stand. This boastful lie that has asserted itself above a man has had a rippling effect on their influence. For years, behaviors and words have been picked apart and overanalyzed to death. Men have been scrutinized and put under a microscope. Now, it's "empowering" when a woman wants to lie with as many men as she likes, but it's dog-like for a man. Why? I get it, the tables have turned. For a *long* time, women were the ones under a microscope. They wore the scarlet A for even looking at a man. Why should either man or woman be treated like this?

I went to Kent State University and its sister schools. I often found myself in conversations where I didn't fit the mold. When debating things like feminism, I was frustrated by the definition versus what form it had taken. The origin of feminism was to make room for equality—where women had no voice and no vote. These newer rises of feminism are boastful and seek to assert women above men. When I refer to myself as a feminist, I am referring to the former definition in its true form, not the latter.

What we have done in the US is permitted women to wear the shoes of both a man and woman, acting as sole parent and provider. The woman who gets it catches my drift. It's exhausting to be both a single parent and work. It's exhausting to wear two sets of shoes. We were not made to do it all. Can we? We can, but we will buckle under the weight of it. I'm not stingy in my beliefs as to breadwinner, mother does this, and father that per family. We need not go there—each person is different in how God created them. Family dynamics differ from home to home, but the pressure a woman carries these days is unnecessary.

Men are more than what they can provide. Women are more than what they look like. Rather than looking at the leaves of a plant, why don't we look at the root? The heart posture says it all. Why aren't you a part of your children's lives, Dad? Mom, why do you take the reins refusing a man to help you? Rather than submit to the lie that this is who I am, dig deeper. Get to the roots. Just because it was like that before doesn't mean it will be again. Doing the same thing expecting different results is by definition insanity. We keep exhausting ourselves, thinking this is life. It's not. There is another way. The family unit is vital!

God made you with all the things in mind. He knew you would say or do a thing. The behaviors don't define you, but they do reveal what is in your heart—what your faith is in. Let Him do heart surgery.

Mama, you were the woman for the job before being given the opportunity or the children. Dad, you were the man for the job before being given the task or the child.

Could we go back and let Him define us? We each have a different role and it's not weak. It's not a bad thing that we have our limits. Each shoe is a different size. Theirs doesn't fit you, sis. Hers don't fit you, bro. Ask the Lord what you were made for, but before even diving into the purpose, get to know the Designer of the purpose.

Who were you made for? Seeking this question first will guide every other effort.

Everything is birthed from faith. What you believe will naturally exude from your thoughts, words, and behaviors. What do you believe about you? What does God say of you? do they oppose one another? Why? Our place is rest, so why does our life look so chaotic? Let the Lord reveal to you the roots that are beneath the surface of your behaviors.

Is He bringing to remembrance any roots?

_____

_____

_____

_____

_____

_____

———————

You are Lord

THIS PIECE WAS WRITTEN AT the beginning of 2022, and so much has changed since. In two years, I've gotten to know God as Lord in and through my life.

It's common practice for me to ask how someone first knew the Lord. Was He introduced as a healer, peacemaker, redeemer, or friend? I've had this revelation for some time that I am settled with calling God Papa, Father, Redeemer, Friend, all the things except Lord. Lord is tricky for me because to be Lord over my life I'd have to fully surrender pain and trust that He is good. Having gone through injustices of all kinds from my upbringing, to my marriage, and finally the loss of my children, some roots began to take form questioning, "Are You still good?" Each time I loosen the reigns and give Him control, He shows up and blows the lid off my expectations. When we go through so much heartache and loss, our mind expects the worst, and meeting Him at His promises becomes a war against flesh and mind. We think "I've done this thing alone for a bit and I'm still alive" rather than "if I would just rely on You, I'd be walking in Your promises and in my calling." Can you see the other side as roots begin to lift and new life begins?

No matter your circumstances, what you've done, or what pain has been done to you, God sees you. That thing that comes to mind, be it abuse, rape, violence, unforgiveness, all of it—that thing hurt God too. Remember that. God always makes a way out. (1 Corinthians 10:13) He sees and hears you, and He IS FOR YOU! (Isaiah 42:3)

Take heart, He loves and wants you, not because of anything you've said or done or avoided saying or doing. We take our ashes in exchange for His beauty. You don't earn any of it. You can't perform well enough to deserve His love or mercy.

I've made plenty of mistakes. My broken cup has been full of many things besides God, but I know that His grace is sufficient. He does not remove His love from me when times get tough. He leads me and guides me. When I stumble, like a child learning to walk, He is there to pick me up, dust me off, and tell me He is proud of me. God is SO good. Remember, when He made you, He said you are "very good." (Genesis 1:31) You are worthy of love because only the creator can decide what their creation is worth! You are not just worthy of love, you already have it freely given.

Royalty

EVERYTHING GOD MADE WAS GOOD, including people. In Genesis, when He made man, He said it was good. When we doubt who we are and cut ourselves down with our words, we slay a unique expression of our Father. Our Heavenly Father's understanding is not our own nor anyone's we have met. We are made in His image, but we are not Him. When we look at a person's failings or abandonment, we can't put that on God. He will never leave us or abandon us. He is for us.

It's important to remember that in our weakness He is made strong and that we can do all things through His strength, not our own. We are not God. We can never strive enough to rely on our own authority in and over our lives. His Word remains the firm foundation, and we trust because we know His character. So then why do we toil over ourselves thinking we must be the exception to His love, promise, and favor? We are good because God said we were made good. We don't have to earn goodness or prove it. We already are. It's in knowing who we are in Him that we can stand with authority as a child of God, a child of the King.

What does it matter that enemies throw rocks at your windows? You live in the palace, and the world is yours. You are worth believing in. Believe in you. God does.

No Invitation Needed

I'M NOT GOING TO INVITE You in. I'm not going to wait for a sign. You go before me and behind me because you are indefinitely invited with an automatic door. Make a scene. Show out. Do Your will because my door is always open. Expectation drives miracles, doesn't it? It is faith for what you already know. If He did it before, He will do it again. The Holy Spirit never leaves me nor forsakes me, so then I know He does not depart from me. I don't have to invite Him into a setting whether with family, friends, or strangers. I already know that He goes with me wherever I go, and it is electricity running through me. He can light up any given room He wants to, and I am His doorway.

Surrender is to yield, to back off from our own ways and allow His. Do that. Stop asking permission from your Father for things that have remained true from the beginning of time. Declare with assurance that you are His daughter or son.

"Or what man is there among you who, if his son asks for bread, will give him a stone? Or if he asks for a fish, will he give him a serpent?" (Matthew 7:7–12)

When was the last time you recall a princess or prince begging for something? Deceleration means to make known, set forth, or explain. It's an acknowledgment of something that is. It's already yours. You are a joint heir to the throne. What is the King's is yours. Do you not perceive it?

"The Spirit Himself bears witness with our spirit that we are children of God, and if children, then heirs—heirs of God and joint heirs with Christ, if indeed we suffer with Him, that we may also be glorified together." (Romans 8:16–17)

New Garments

YOU GET ENTANGLED WITH BROKEN people, forgetting that you are whole. It's like the fabric of your wholeness becomes stretched and begins tearing the seams like a beautifully fashioned garment that's being pulled off you by the beggars around you. You are like an Elizabethan woman with ruffles and curls, but when you don't know your authority and walk down the broken streets, all the beggars you see yourself in yearn for and beg for what you carry all while you are entirely oblivious.

If you knew what you carried and who you belonged to, you could continue to give to the broken without allowing them to steal from you. You could walk with the confidence of royalty, offering to give and support without becoming like the common folk. It's not to say you would yield an air about you or that you would be seated above anyone, but your identity is royalty and demands respect and authority. It is a presence that changes the room rather than being swayed by all the beggars walking by.

Quit offering your riches to those with a poverty mindset. As long as their mindset is set on squandering what blessing they have, they aren't for you. God will heal and repair you if you allow Him to. Then, He will bring you a partner of equal stature, equal presence, and equal authority to work hand in hand as He has called you. Yes,

He is aware of what you are attracted to. It's not all kingdom mentality. He cares about what you care about and the little things. He also knows what makes you feel safe, seen, wanted, respected, and overall loved.

If you don't know who you are, you won't walk like it. What you are confident in speaks for itself. I have given my heart to those who sought only to use it for personal gain. I didn't understand the importance of hiding my heart in Him so that the wrong person or the wrong timing didn't cause distraction or unnecessary pain. God is the only one who truly knows another man's heart.

"But the Lord said to Samuel, 'Do not look at his appearance or at his physical stature, because I have refused him. For the Lord does not see as man sees; for a man looks at the outward appearance, but the Lord looks at the heart." (1 Samuel 16:7)

The issues of life flow from the heart, and if we give our heart at the wrong time, having unhealed or dealt with heartache and pain, we will hurt ourselves and cut the receiving person on all that broken glass. Likewise, if we don't understand the order of this life with God being the foundation, we can be quick to make a man or woman our idol. Statements like "you are my everything" or "I couldn't live without you" seem sweet and enticing but reveal a sinister posture as they've just confessed you are God to them or that you've made them God.

Beautiful princess or prince, know your worth by knowing whose you are first and then who you are so that you don't drop the crown. Keep your head held high and fixed to the Son. He will help you grow, and you will learn the ropes of what it means to be righteous, to fully submit to His authority and walk like you believe it.

The Scripture in 1 Samuel points to Lord, not Alpha, Omega, or Jehovah Rapha. Why is it *Lord* in this passage? *Lord* means "master" in Hebrew and points to an ultimate authority. The Lord is our authority. He has the final say. His way is not our own, and His vantage point is different from ours. He sees the heart while we see outward appearance. Even with spiritual eyes, we only see in part. "For we know in part and we prophecy in part." (1 Corinthians 13:9)

God gives us insight to know what to stand for in prayer, in agreement with His Word. He doesn't show us something about someone to share with the class. He shares because He trusts us with that information. What are we doing with it? We must understand that He knows best. It is His will and not our own. He knows your heart and theirs. His ways are not ours, and His thoughts are not ours. Be sure and submit your thoughts and your heart to Him so that you can stand confidently in who He is and what He says about you.

Think of a time when you may have cheapened yourself or given
your heart away at the wrong time? What did you learn?
What does God say about it?

_____
_____
_____
_____
_____
_____
_____
_____
_____
_____

Then What?

I'VE NEVER BEEN A GO-WITH-THE-FLOW sort of girl. I'm the one who brings a fat checklist and packs anything one can muster up as a "what if." That's me. Hi, let me introduce the sting of anxiety. The problem is, it doesn't fit into God's plan. He wants your trust and manages the lists and "ifs" because He knows the what. Have you ever seen a trust fall exercise? The thought of that used to make me quite tense. No thank you. Surely, they will drop me.

I accepted the Lord when I was a little girl and saw things others didn't as I was given new eyes. I had a magnetic love inside of me that drew friends and adults who would spill their hearts with ease. The light draws insects too, and I couldn't tell their form, or maybe I played God and thought I'd save them rather than pointing them to the Son. I believed I could stick them in a jar and carry them around, but then I'd find bugs in my bed. I didn't change them. They changed me.

What we believe will manifest, and so faith is tested. Let's see what you really believe. We are all tested to be refined as gold. In Job, we read, "But He knows the way I take; When He has tried me, I shall come forth as gold."

Gold is already gold before hitting the flame. The flame is meant to refine. Study yourself approved. Get to know the Lord and His goodness so that you can pass the test and make a testimony as it was always meant to be. Don't take a page from Bob the Builder's book. We don't need more walls. We need more hearts. In all your ways acknowledge Him and He will give you direction. Seek first the kingdom of God. Don't you want to know who you are and where you came from? The more you know who you are, the more you act like it. The walls will fall down. Give everything, good, bad, and ugly to God. He knows, and He still loves you—not despite those things but because He made someone beautiful.

Whose Voice?

THIS VOICE IN MY HEAD gets loud, GETS LOUDER. Whose voice has to shout to be heard? My God speaks quietly, and He knows what He is worth. I settle in to hear His voice, silence the chaos, and forget all the noise. His voice finds me in the pockets of my day as I tune in to a frequency that doesn't ask the demands of this world. Whose voice bellows loudly? Shouting and angry—fiery darts that you'll never quite earn. Just one taste. Lord knows that you've earned...earning. That's just noise—not for me.

My Father's voice is lovely, and He yearns for a relationship. Never needing a thing—just the simplicity of our hearts. Who said you couldn't leap like the beasts in the field? Who said you couldn't climb the trees? Who said that your hands couldn't make beautiful things? Who said that you could not go somewhere new and become something different from the shame you put on?

Take it off. Take off those words you put on—those dank clothes—they're all wrong for you. Your crown has fallen to the gutters. Yours is the kingdom. The last I checked, your blood was royal. Who said? Who cares? Your Father is King, and what He says goes.

You cannot earn what your Father freely gave you. He tore the veil so that you would be in perfect union with Him, grafting you into His bloodline. His blood is your own so that all that is His is yours. Are you not a royal priesthood? Are you not a joint heir to His throne? Do you believe it? Do you see what He sees? You are made in His image? Yes, and you are royal. Yes, you are the head, not the tail. Yes, you are a creator because He created. Yes, you are a mother or a father. Yes, you are capable because "I can do all things through Christ who strengthens me." (Philippians 4:13) It is in Him that you find who you are. It is in your weakness you reach out and ask Him to do it. Help me! Who are You? I want to know You.

Answer the following questions using "I am" and "He is" statements. For example: *2 Corinthians 5:21—"For He made Him who knew no sin to be sin for us, that we might become the righteousness of God in Him." I am the righteousness of God. Christ paid a heavy price for my freedom by shedding royal blood, the blood of great authority, the only authority. He is Lord.*

Who is the Lord? It is written…

_____

_____

_____

_____

_____

_____

Who are You? It is written...

The Lion's Voice

WHAT IS THE CHARACTER OF a lion? I'm not talking about the cooped-up zoo lion who has learned not to bite the hand that feeds it. I'm referencing the mighty African lion with a ferocious mane, sharp daunting teeth, and a voice that pierces the stillness throughout the entire kingdom. In the jungle or across the African plains, the lion is alpha. Alpha begins the Greek alphabet as its first letter, meaning first. He leads the pack with authority. No other beast dare come against him or one of his cubs. They may well become lunch.

I grew up with a language that belittled the authority and strength of God—"God, please do Your will...if you will it." That language precedes doubts about His ability to deliver. Somehow religion erased the identity of the Lion in the depiction of the Lion and the Lamb. Without the Lion, we erase authority, dominion, power, reign, and the fight He so freely gives us, vindicating the righteousness of His children.

This God who laid the foundations of the earth is not weak, but when we take a look at Christians who don't know the countenance of the great Lion they serve, the image we have of Christ is weakened. Unless we take up our authority and yield our weapon boldly, we identify with fear, barring us from the fullness of who God is. Suddenly, those with impossible situations start to question whether God can handle them. This God, the one true God, breathed life into every blade of grass, every set of lungs. He spoke and life began! What a mighty God we serve, but this reverence is necessary. Obedience is necessary. We can become haphazardly dependent on a genie God whom we only rely on when we want something so then many of us don't truly seek Him until in a desperate state and hungry for freedom. Having a healthy reverence or great respect and honor for this Lion is everything.

If you were to visit a king in the castle, surely you would understand the honor to behold such royalty and authority. The exciting part of God's royal bloodline is that you belong to it. When your heart posture is honor and respect, you align more naturally with the kingdom of God and with wisdom and clarity. If you were to ask your Father, the King, a request, you come to Him with humility and confidence knowing He is for you and knows what is best for you. What He says is not void but fulfilled in this thematic kingdom—trusting most of us have not grown up in a castle or around royals. What the King says goes, period. Let His Word cut down every boasting tree and protect those that are His—that's all of us. Let the lion roar!

A Roaring Voice

I'VE HAD A SONG IN my mouth from a young age with this passion to connect others through music, but my understanding of worship and praise was not always as it is now. I used to feel safe behind the restriction of closed eyes, arms to the side, and smashed behind a pew. God forbid, I hit the wrong note. I didn't understand what it meant to worship in spirit and in truth, to cause my body to be recklessly abandoned by the Spirit of God, and to worship and praise Him publicly as I did in private. When I praise at home, you can hear my old 1800s floors creaking along as I jump up and down with the beat. I dance as the Spirit moves, and there was no chain on me due to no viewers being around. The opinion of others was the looming authority that blotted out the freedom I had in song.

We worship Him with our voice, but we also worship Him with our lives. Our lives are a reflection of our heart posture. Is it fixed on Him, submitted to Him? What are we speaking and doing behind closed doors? That is a good indication of what our lives look like worshipping God.

There is so much truth in beauty for ashes, in the great exchange—in joy for mourning. I won't lie to you and tie a ribbon around my life as if I've perfected the walk, but on the days that I can wrap my head around this reckless surrender, I am blessed. I stop the fictitious arguments in my mind and the accusatory words that creep up to remind me of who I am not. During these times of surrender, I learn to praise in the aching, lifting Him up as the One who can do exceedingly abundantly more than I.

We all know that our daddy's shoes do not fit us. We couldn't bear a moment trying to lift one of those shoes a millimeter, let alone comprehend as He does. The peace is in the release. Some of these situations we experience are "impossible" by the world's standards. Just because there is a history of this way doesn't mean God won't do it a new way. Just because it's never been done, doesn't mean it won't be done now.

Think about Moses and the parting of the Red Sea. Can you imagine coming against thunderous waves and the sound of clanging metal armor and many horses headed right toward you? That would be enough for anyone to doubt God, but He parted the waters and overcame their enemies. There is always room for a "But God" in our lives.

Power lives and breathes on our tongues. If we trust the Lord in our hearts, the words that flow from our lips reflect that heart posture. Then, we can create or we can tear down. Let's avoid the latter. Do you think it's a coincidence how many children have ended their lives over words? No, words have power. In the beginning, God spoke and what happened? Life formed. If we want to see the "impossible" happen in our lives, let's not create more hurdles by using our tongues to cut down ourselves or anyone else. Let us use our tongues to lift up a shout of praise or spend intimate time in worship. He deserves all the praise and worship. For without Him, who would we be?

Without Him, what would this world look like? So go on, break off the restraints that hold you from singing like you want to, from praying like you ache to, from making an absolute fool of yourself for God. Love looks quite foolish on the outside, doesn't it? But inside, we are bursting with life and joy. Pearls are formed by irritation. Sometimes the very thing set to burn out your light causes you to adjust why you burned in the first place. You may have flickered for a while, but now you have become used to the dark and it doesn't scare you. It won't overcome you, and you shine that much brighter!

All of the Glory is Yours

DO YOU EVER LATCH ONTO a word and wonder, "What does that actually mean?" I started inquiring about the Hebrew or Greek context of a word years ago and only invested greater time more recently. What does *glory* mean? Glory comes from the Hebrew word *Kavod* meaning honor or respect, weight. If we give glory to the Father, what does He want from us that would be worth giving to such a BIG God?

When honoring and respecting someone in authority, especially the military, you quiet yourself and listen to who is in charge, obeying their words. You know that there is an order of authority with a general, lieutenant general, major general, brigadier general, colonel, and the list goes on.

We honor and respect the Lord with our lives as a living sacrifice. No, we don't have to earn or strive our way into something freely given, but we naturally exude what we believe. What we are confident in shows. When we make God the Lord over our lives, then we obey what He says. We no longer argue over the matter because we understand that we are arguing with the Almighty God. A natural reverence exists retaining our humility. There exists a rank.

What a strong leader says carries weight. A leader is someone whom others look to for guidance, and when they speak, others take note. When the teacher is teaching, the student is learning and listening. Notes are taken on matters to help them study and apply those lessons for a later need. What we make mental note of bears weight, and its repeated loop in our minds reflects the authority we have given it.

We glorify the Lord with our lives laid down before Him. We listen and obey. The weight of who we are is given up to the Lord as we give Him our burdens to carry. We exchange our burdens for His peace knowing that, when He asks a thing of us, He has the best for us. As a joint heir, we learn what it means to have authority. Old patterns fall away as we apply truth, and the more time we spend with Him, the more we look like Him. When a king is being raised up, they don't live like the rest of the village. Yes, there are certain privileges, but the life comes with a certain weight to it. An entire village will one day look to him for solutions. If you are leaning on your own understanding and not submitting to God's Word in obedience, you not only fall under the weight of it but mislead those around you.

I look back at patterns of behavior I had that likely confused people around me. I would believe one thing and live entirely differently. That's what it means to be double-minded. I could know all the things but not apply them. Did I really know them then or did I know of them? When you know a thing, your life will follow suit to exemplify it naturally. If it's just lip service, that much is apparent to everyone around you. Faith without works... (James 2:17) Hearer of the Word and not a doer... (James 1:22) We hear the Word and don't apply it, because the seed falls on another type of ground, not good soil. (Matthew 13:18–23) A hardened heart will often shut out truth because it is too focused on the hurt or the pain to receive anything but that.

Being double-minded sounds an awful lot like ADHD. I once heard it said that ADHD is having all the resources and no application (or something to that effect). I'm not dogging you if you have been diagnosed with ADHD as I also took medication for some time for ADHD and for PTSD. I just stopped vilifying it in my mind and realized, even if I have a tendency to do a thing, I don't need to necessarily identify with it. The culture we live in succumbs to identifying with everything under the sun. We've got bumper stickers to boast in our travels, stickers plastered all over our water bottles, jewelry, and signs in our homes. The market is saturated with an identity crisis. I don't want to be a Debby Downer, because that's not what I'm going for here. Identifying with two opposing things just splits our mind. It shows that we don't know what we want. If we are getting plastered every weekend and then praising the Lord on Sunday, it shows we are not clear about who we are and what we believe. I'm speaking from a place of love and experience. I used to do just that.

What we believe is apparent in how we live our lives, but our behaviors also do not demand our identity. We are who He says we are. The behaviors are just patterns we have become accustomed to. As we believe what He says, those things will fall away because we start to crave differently. No longer does the drink satisfy or fill the void. No longer does sex cover the intimacy you desire. We lay our lives down to the Lord as He gets all the glory in the heart and character shift. When looking at a person who used to spend every day getting high to a person who is now present and no longer craving those things, only God gets the glory. You catch my drift? When the impossible becomes possible, it becomes a testimony and now the witnesses want to know how. Really, they want to know Who.

Let's put a little weight behind who we are talking to and what He says. He is Alpha and Omega, beginning and the end. Take in

His reverence. He is in every cell and atom. He breathed life into the trees, the bark, and its roots. He tells the wind which way it should blow. He created each species in vast waters and the ecosystem it belongs to. He designed you and knitted you together in your mother's womb. (Psalm 139:13)

"But we all, with unveiled face, beholding as in a mirror the glory of the Lord, are being transformed into the same image from glory to glory, just as by the Spirit of the Lord." (2 Corinthians 3:18)

Faith Is Not for the Weak

HAVING FAITH IN WHAT LOOKS impossible, against all odds—every word of hope seemingly defeated and memories dwindling—is *rough*. Do you know what it is to cry out to the Lord for what you believe to be your portion—often feeling like a dream you buried a long time ago? Do you know what it is to hunger and thirst for justice, for connection with what is yours?

Faith begins as a seed, but it doesn't remain in seed form. It is watered and nurtured to life until it begins to sprout and take form. Soon its roots are deeply planted and unshakable. No matter the rains that dare to pull her from her roots, none can as the surface reveals what looks like an iceberg. She is more than petals and leaves. Her roots sink deep into the earth, drinking from a well that NEVER runs dry. If for a moment you believe faith could be stomped out, you'll find an entire forest behind her. The sun and the soil, the winds and the rains all belong to her. None can shake her.

Sunflowers start as dainty leafy plants, delicate and small, and they can grow to the boastful size of six feet tall. They are crushed to produce oil and sustenance. As with their impressive height, their provision yields nourishment for all types of creatures, making the plant an integral part of its environment. Sunflowers spend the majority of their life facing the sun, and without it, it withers away. Although their start is insignificant, soon they grow resilient against extreme heat and dryness, defying its conditions. They are dedicated, strong, and joyous.

You, my dear friend, are a sunflower. A crushing is often needed to produce oil in our lives. That oil is needed to sustain us through the harshest of times. It is like sunshine in the dark places for those around you. Your pursuant nature reflects the purpose and intention of a sunflower.

Shine on, dear sunflower. Keep growing tall, and take a look in the mirror. My, have you grown.

Can't Leave You at Home

I CAN'T HEAR YOUR VOICE when I'm listening to my own.
I can't face my giants when I try to do it alone.
I can't leave Your spirit at home.
You go with me, before me, beside me all the same.
You call me wanted, chosen; You know my true name.
So I'll shout it from my lowest place,
and I'll dress Your name in praise.
My mountain has no other fame,
just beauty in the rain.

Daughter, lovely, I'm proud of who you are.
You may fall, but I've had you from the start.
There's no valley I can't reach you.
There's no mountain too big for teaching.
You are grace, and you are light.
You're never beyond My sight.
Even darkness cannot take you,
because My plans, you know, they're for you.

Reflection

THERE SHE SAT, AT ATTENTION for the world's viewing, sixteen years of age. Like a wind-up toy awaiting play time, she looked at the boys with apprehension, for she knew and deeply understood their affections for her—their coveted imaginations dancing behind eyelids. She was the life of the party, stories circulating this way and that as if she had some dark secret hidden away inside her—like a treasure. She resembled other girls with tight curls, lips painted in ravishing reds, materials that hugged her body just so and mimicked the touch of love she desired. The girl found an opening she could force herself through, standing, waiting for her crowd's affirmation, an approval that never quite filled the void within her own heart. And each night she found pleasure in a man she thought she knew—a man who was much like the others—a figure of momentary comfort, fleeting penetration.

Across from the girl of her youth sat her double, at the age of twenty-four, still bearing light's budding flower perhaps, hanging on words of hope, desperately as each thread had relinquished its grip on her soul. At times, she glanced at her reflection of girlhood, masked womanhood, with rage warring in her heart for she longed to shake the girl into perception, into clarity. "Wake up?" She would yell across the room whereby the girl did not reply for her ears had been deafened from truth. With age, with growth, she believed she had uncovered truth and awoke from the darkness she was blanketed in for so long.

Reality has a way of inviting herself in, revealing the illusions all women walk in. The woman stood up and began running toward her ghost, but a mirror caught her grip and shattered at her embrace. And with shards of glass, the reflections cut her to pieces, waking the sleeper of the past.

Her daughter burst in, and it jolted her from thought. Her bouncing yellow curls and bright baby blues flickering sunshine as if she could smile with her eyes. (Every time she climbs in the car, she asks for "This Little Light of Mine" as she sings with such tenderness pouring from her heart.) She brushed her hands against a tube of mascara and lipstick, diving right into the brushes still tinged with grains of mineral. Oh, how she longed to be like her mother, beautiful and put together. She reached over to one of the brushes and swept it across her cheek, proudly glancing over to see if her mother had noticed. (She too was once a little girl, one who was always revered for her doll-like beauty so much that she became dull, lifeless with a painted-on face, just so that the world beheld her as such.) Her gaze was fixed upon her daughter once more, and she considered her eyes, hearing her daughter's words as tangible as day, whispered in her heart, "Mommy, I want to be just like you."

This piece was written during my time in college. It was originally published in Volume 26 of Kent State's literary journal, *Canto*. My ex-husband and I had both submitted two pieces to be accepted, and both were anonymously selected and published.

At the time, I was exchanging classes and assignments for accusation and torment in a courtroom, parenting classes, and house calls from the state that never warranted a cause given we didn't have a single visit with our children. This was written as a response to considering who I felt I was at the moment versus my teenage years and growing up. I was sitting in bed looking at my vanity writing and replaying a memory of my daughter Neya coming into my room as I was finishing up getting ready for the day. It reveals my heart posture in the moment. Looking back at now thirty years old, I'm becoming the woman of God I always longed to be. I feared my daughter walking the same path I did, seeking approval from people. I was terrified that she would cheapen herself to what everyone else said of her. I saw the beauty in all that she was and her curiosity and hunger for innocence and joy. My heart was that she would retain it and that it wouldn't be stolen.

I needed to include this piece because this woman is not who she once was. When I look in the mirror now, I see everything I was made to be, defined by and adored by my Maker, I see my heart. It is my hope that you too would see your reflection as God made you and you would see Him in you.

Worn

I'VE LEARNED THAT WHAT COMPLETES the outfit isn't the pattern, cost, brand, or layer, nor the way it folds, hugs, grips, or lays. It is the confidence one wields in being true. No matter how a dress drapes across her shoulders or the way a high heel lengthens the legs, if the woman adorned is not confident in her own presence, the fabric becomes drab.

Then, living simply becomes reality as we retain the pieces that help us reflect the confidence we already have and we throw out those purchased for someone we never were.

What we are confident in shows.

You. You. You.

IDENTITY IS THE SOURCE OF who you are, and our culture wars for your identity. Isn't that the true war? We are pulled in a thousand directions as we are marketed to, pulling for attention, investment, and eventual heart and identity.

As a woman, I've been called a lot of things, and focusing on those words can be debilitating. They were never meant to have power and authority in our lives. No matter how much a man tells me I am beautiful and everything they ever wanted, they fumble the ball. Never commit. The heart is not to be trifled with, played with like a toy, but it must be hidden in Christ—guarded at all times.

A treasure is hidden for a reason. We are compared to diamonds, pearls, rubies, and gold. These are all precious and costly. That is what a treasure is composed of—precious things. We are made with an insatiable hunger only God can fill, and He made marriage. When a woman does not look in the mirror and see Christ, she cheapens herself and suddenly sells herself for a cocktail at the bar and maybe a call back. A man who doesn't see Christ in his mirror will not garnish the respect he longs for by how many notches he has collected on his belt. We only look like what we spend time with. If we are not spending time with the Lord, it shows.

No longer are we satisfied with the Lord, letting Him fill the voids, but we seek it out in a man or woman. This option is so costly. We pay for chaos in the form of insecurity, shame, and emptiness. We have to be filled up so that our Christ-sized void is not filled by something that will never fill it. Even a marriage won't do that. God is Alpha and Omega, the beginning and end. He is the start and the finish. Our end goal cannot be a person or they become an idol. We will put pressure on a man or woman who cannot fulfill that obligation. We are meant to come into marriage both being full of the Lord so that both walk hand in hand, loving and supporting one another in their purpose(s).

Ladies, when we are hidden in Him, only he with instruction can find us. He has to hear from the Lord to find his gem. Confidence is quiet. (Notice I didn't say silent.) These very words I am currently typing once offended my heart, but truth is offensive. Do we want to be bitter or better? Let offense be like a check engine light. A check engine light alerts the owner of a vehicle that it needs to go into the shop to uncover the problem under the hood. When the check engine light (offense) comes up in your heart, ask yourself why am I feeling this way? Our portion is peace, so if we don't have it, we must ask God why.

A man is called to love his wife as the church, and he cannot do so without first having love. If He does not know the love of God, he cannot give you what you are after. God gives man and woman a void only He can fill so that we come to Him for perfect union where both husband and wife honor one another while also honoring God. It makes a strong foundation for child-rearing—a team of two on the same side. It's the way God designed it.

Discover who you are in the Lord. You will find Him when you seek Him with your whole heart. When you want something bad enough, you'll do anything to get it. Have you ever had a crush you liked so much that you would do anything for him or her to notice you? If we can give that sort of attention to a human, surely we give much more to the King of Kings and Lord of Lords. You'll find you when you find Him. Find Him, and taste that He is good. Now ask who He says you are. You believe Him because you know Him. Now move when He says move. When your heart's desires line up with His, He blesses you with what your heart desires. You start to look like Him. At this point, your identity looks more like God and reflects your true nature which attracts the right person. You want someone who is after the heart of God too, because if you take the turkey out before it is done cooking, it is raw and causes sickness.

Find Him. Find you. All else will fall into place.

––––––––––––

Naked Truth

ALL MY HEART IS IN this stuff,
remains in a closet collecting dust.
Something that made me feel seen,
a strappy top or ripped-up jeans.
Each item with a story to tell
of a way I danced or the way I felt.
Like photographs hold memories,
my laughs and cries are woven in costumery.
Each one of them is another part of me,
a lazy bum or high society.
Frolicking child, dancing down the street.
Keep your eyes wide open and notice me!
I wish it were that simple,
a cry for a stare, a look, or a glare.
But these things hold me captive
because I hate the feeling of being bare.
Being naked to who I am,
the truth of my failings, the masks that I wear.
They're more than comfort and threads sewn together.

More than something to keep away cold weather.
These patterns and buttons come alive on my skin,
drenched in the beauty I've found in them.

Shine On!

A SONG FOR MY DAUGHTERS with sunshine hair.
You've got sunshine in your hair.
You've got light within your eyes,
And if only you knew just how bright you shine.
All the world is yours to take.
Full adventure, pave a way.
Look to where your help comes from.
You're His daughter—you're enough!
And on those days when life gets heavy,
Know, baby, you're always with me.
You've got sunshine in your hair.
You've got light within your eyes.
And if only you knew just how bright you shine.
Keep on shining. Keep on shining. Keep on shining.
They need your light.
So let your light shine on and light up the darkness.
With God as your fortress and friend,
Shine on. Shine on. Shine on. Shine on. Shine on.
Keep on shining. Keep on shining.
Your light is like a lamp unto their feet.
You've got sunshine in your hair.
You've got light within your eyes.
And if only you knew just how bright you shine.

Prisoner of the Mind

OUR MINDS CAN INCRIMINATE THE most innocent of us, asking in circles; throw away the key—this is a life sentence, and no one to plea. Moving images, clanging noises indoctrinate the youth—causing us to freeze in time, powerless to move, you are mine. Our voice is the breakthrough we have buried inside. We spend a lifetime trying to hide. Precious things hide beneath the surface untainted by the pirates of change. Dig a little deeper; you are sure to hit treasure. It's not easy to find. I beg you let me out of these shackles. I bellow Scripture to remind You of what You said. Really, I remind myself. I'm enamored by this thing called love. What makes you want me? This question plagues my mind, a hungry little thing and devouring thoughts always gnawing for more—an insatiable hunger. She plays nasty tricks on me. I renew her day by day. This conformity is not for me—a trial for the blind. Teach me Your ways. I submit my mind.

Industry Standard

YOU TOLD ME THAT I spoke too softly to garnish respect and that all of the men in the room just wouldn't let up on maintaining control unless I spoke up. But little did I know the small women around me breathed fear down my back, telling me I ought to stand up and not hold back. Now they say I'm too loud. We just won't have that. So which is it I say, speak louder or softer, remain silent and put us under or risk losing it all?

What if I fall? Will you be there to pick me back up, love me despite it all? I don't think so—that's my downfall. See, I've never battled men in this allusive need for control. It's been you all along reminding me I'm not enough. Well, I am here to call your bluff!

The truth, I'll tell you—It's a facade. You've taught me to glue my mask on tight and puff up my chest; yeah, that looks alright. Never good enough to stand on my own, but pathetic enough to give a man a home. Hmm…that's ironic. You painted your face, so you're on it. Always spinning webs to catch your prey. But the biggest joke, hey, I gotta say it, is us women who let you rob our light, buying fake advertisements—don't be so uptight. We'll never live up to this lie you've become because even you don't believe it. You yourself are numb.

I won't sell myself short, not any longer. You've duped others for years, but my dear, I am stronger because I know it is He from where my help comes from. I don't need your fake news, so move on along. This industry needs a shake-up at best. Wake up, ladies, come on and get dressed! Dress yourself with truth and grace. I know you're tired of running this race. Get off the track, and dust off your shoes. God has a new purpose, and He is calling after you!

Humble Pie

TODAY GOD ASKED ME TO recall all the ways He has been good to me to remind me of who He is and, by extension, who I am in Him. The Creator of the universe lives in me, and I often forget that. How do I forget something so life-changing, so impactful? It's easy to become distracted. For me, I get stuck scrolling or binging, anything to live vicariously through someone else, most of the time fictional characters. Boy, do I get sucked into the drama. I can be found on my couch yelling at the man who did her wrong or crying at the heartache and loss, and it isn't even real! It's easier to be vulnerable in the comfort of my living room without having to expose my heart to another or face the music, sometimes heart-wrenching, sometimes joyful.

I think it's obvious why we avoid pain, but why avoid joy? I often avoid the joy too because I'm afraid it will be taken from me, so I avoid it altogether. This way, I avoid losing something precious.

As I think about all the ways God has been good to me, I silence myself. I steady my breath. I remove the distracting thoughts as I picture exhaling anything that is not associated with God. There are sixteen names of God for minimal purposes. Obviously, God cannot be contained by sixteen definitive names. He is Alpha and Omega, beginning and the end, Creator, Redeemer, and there is too much to contain. Many of the names we draw on regularly like Jehovah Jireh are linked to a song that lives rent-free inside my mind. Jehovah Jireh means "the Lord will provide." I cannot put into words the provision God has supplied in my life.

As I was looking for examples, a few names I didn't see as applicable to use for an example, but I'm going to use one anyway. El Shaddai or "All-sufficient One" didn't feel applicable to my life, because I struggle with finding what is sufficient in God, whether it be grace, healing, power, or love. Sadly, He has not been my number one source. But the more I reflect on how He has been sufficient for me, though I don't always run to Him as my source, He is El Shaddai too! Who He is isn't determined by what we can and cannot see. He is the great "I Am," and His ways are often made known after the fact.

A visiting pastor came to Elevation, my church, to share a message called "I am Number Twelve." In his message, the pastor spoke about the story in Matthew where Peter walked on water. He noted that when Peter saw Jesus, Peter asked if it was Him. Though the man had followed Jesus all this time, had broken bread with Him, trusted Him, and was mentored by Him, he and the other disciples thought Jesus may well be a ghost. The pastor added that often we misjudge something in the middle of the storm that later we recognize as God. He said, "God does not always look like God in the middle of the storm." We might not see what He is doing, but His character is not determined by what we may be blind to in the moment.

Another name is Jehovah Shalom, meaning "The Lord is peace." Ever since my first encounter with God in the woods at Camp Wanake, I knew God as peace. My first introduction to God continues to ground me when I've exhausted myself with anxiety, fear, anger, or whatever other emotion I let run me. I'm sharing my encounters I have with God as an example of His goodness in my life but also to remind myself of all the ways He has been good to me.

When I thought all hope was lost after losing my children, God provided and supplied me with peace. My husband and I chose to part ways and get a divorce after considering the ways that our marriage was not healthy and after I did some soul searching and realized I couldn't fully trust him with the choices he made. I was mourning the loss of my children, my marriage, my innocence (having shared a man I thought was mine and having made choices of my own after the marriage dissolved), and, what felt like at the time, my sanity. But God was there. God knew that I would continue to try to reconcile with my ex-husband and we would become pregnant, He knew I'd lose my children, and He knew that He would redeem me, bring forth truth, and reunion.

Emerson, my son I became pregnant with, was the ultimate blessing that God used to keep pressing me toward the purpose He has for my life. He is part of the reason for breath in my lungs. That may sound dramatic, and it is. I sat in the hospital room, waiting for what felt inevitable, the loss of yet another child, all on the basis of the "Accuser." But God. I sat in that room with devastating cries that bellowed from inside. When I think back on that day, I can hear and feel that moment. It felt like standing at the edge of death and inviting defeat. It felt like being wrapped up in all the lies that were spoken over me, choking the very last breath from my chest. It felt utterly hopeless. I held a child who I thought would not know me and to whom I would say goodbye to. But God. He was and is my peace!

Going back to the message at church, it reflected the heart of God. The pastor said that we, the twelfth disciple, speaking in relation to Peter, are water walkers. What others would drown in, God would have us walk on. When I hear this word, it empowers me to stay the course because God brought me through what I could've drowned in. He had a purpose on the other side, and I couldn't see He was there. That day in the hospital, I looked at my ex-husband and told him that I was done and I was ready to end things. I knew he felt the same, and I had all the courage in the world to go to the roof and carry it out. But God had other plans. My ex called my family to come stay with me, and though I remained depressed and helpless, I had family to support me and give me hope. God worked through my ex to save my life.

Another name that has been revealed in my life is Jehovah Tsidkenu or "The Lord, our righteousness." After moving to Washington state and being given the opportunity to prove myself against the accusations made in Ohio, I was given full rights to my son, and the lies were shattered. They still try to assert themselves in my heart and mind, but they are under my feet in Jesus's name! I am made righteous, which translates to "that which is upright" in Hebrew. I am the head, not the tail. God took what was made to shame and condemn and silenced it, causing me to be upright because He is my righteousness. The word *righteous* means "that which is just and fair."

In a short timeframe, I was able to think on ways God has been good to me without any restraint or need to process. Those are only the ways that come to mind in the moment as I write. There are more, especially after I began to see Him move in my life in miraculous ways. In those times, His ways are even more apparent. God doesn't change. We do. His character remains steady, and if we allow ourselves to be still, we will know the ways He has been faithful.

Take a moment to write at least three ways God has been good to you and line those ways up with who God is. This exercise will give examples of His character in your life and builds trust in who He is, allowing you to build continual faith.)

_____

_____

_____

_____

_____

_____

_____

_____

_____

_____

Can You Dig It?

In a world full of petals and poise, be a dandelion. They take over a yard in yellow spots, adorning her in a new garment for spring. Children take notice. They gather these perennials, sport them with pride, and offer them as a loving gift to parents and teachers alike. Others scoff at the offering and spray to kill them, rendering them a weed. Dandelions release seeds to the wind, spreading their seeds regardless of the permission of man. Be like a dandelion unapologetically true to your birth form, knowing who you are and whose you are, avoiding the lies telling you that you are a weed.

A dandelion begins with a head full of sunshine, and then it is covered. In the covering, a period of time takes place that looks like nothing is happening, but everything is happening inside. The dandelion dies to itself, and then slowly rebirths with seeds to spread as a child plucks its body and makes a wish. The seeds disperse everywhere, reproducing. This is a picture of testimony! (Search for "slow-motion dandelion transformation.")

Joseph was already chosen, already gold, but he needed to be refined. The three men in the fire too, what happened? They didn't smell like smoke nor did they look like what they'd gone through. Gold only goes to the flame to remove impurities so that it shines even brighter and purer. What you think is the devil is a test to purify you so that your life is a living testimony to God's love. How do we defeat the enemy? Glad you asked, by the blood of the Lamb and the word of our testimony—not loving our lives to death, but submitting them. The test is connected to the testimony.

The wilderness is for purification. A dandelion goes inside itself to be purified and comes out with many seeds (testimonies) to disperse through the wind (the Holy Spirit). Testimony comes from the Hebrew word *aydooth*, meaning to do with the same power and authority.

"Your testimonies I have taken as a heritage forever, for they are the rejoicing of my heart." (Psalm 119:111) Heritage means inheritance. You don't earn it. God already knew you and chose you, knowing what you'd decide, what you'd do and not do. He looks at the heart.

When you pass a test, you can teach that material because you know it. You walk a path so that others can follow behind. This is the life of a forerunner, often overlooked and underqualified. But God, He qualifies the called. He does not call the qualified.

What happened to the three men in the fire when they didn't look like they were testing? Well, it was a table in the presence of their enemies. Your enemies have a choice. They can either watch you eat or see that what you are eating is good and ask for a bite too. How? Only God. Impossible made possible. Even the king who threw the men in the fire believed on this God, the one who caused these men to not be touched by the flame. The fourth man. That voice of authority then shook the nation as the king praised unto the Lord and gave glory to such a God as powerful as theirs. The kingdom followed by example. (Daniel 3:16–30)

Dandelion, don't you think God knew who He was making? He made you a flower regardless of who thinks you're a weed. Your approval comes from the Lord. He who accepts me accepts my Father. Please don't put a hand on me. My God is protective and loving. He is desperate to know every inch of me and of you. Judgment and correction are necessary in the kingdom of God. He has plans to prosper you for a hope and a future. Is it about you? Not really. It's to you through you. It's the point of all eyes seeing who you follow. Our pastor said, "A leader with no followers is just taking a walk." People come in droves to one carrying the light because they ache for love. They ache for joy.

Choice. There is choice. There are consequences, but you are still afforded a seat at the table. Bless those who curse you. Lift them up anyway. Are they not His child too? Let's contend that rather than watch me eat, they'll have a craving for the very wild love I'm eating. What is that? I want that. Yes, a great gathering! Boldly lift your head, dandelion. You were made for such a time as this.

PART TWO

NEW WINE

"You cannot see the wind,
but you can see the product of it.
His Spirit resides in You."
—John 3:8

Where Are My Future Thinkers?

WHERE ARE MY FUTURE THINKERS—THE ones who strive to live in the clouds—far from it all?

I don't live in the past. It's so buried beneath heartache and pain, resistant to touch the sharp shards of glass. I live in a future where continuous planning allows for the constant hum of noise to flood my mind—keeping silent the hurt. In the future, I see joy and laughter; I see promise and life. But the present, I've yet to understand it as a gift. It's one that takes being still and appreciative. There are pockets of sunshine and awakening but mostly a window into reality.

Those who dread what they've done, like a broken record in their minds, continue circling mistakes and misfortune. The present day-ers think for the moment at hand. They leap and laugh, and they live. What is consequence? What is planning? They fly by the seat of their pants. They're the kind a planner could only aspire to be.

There has to be a middle ground, to acknowledge the past and let it go, to take each breath and hold it as sacred, and to yearn for something more. Maybe I have some sort of balance, but it's like ebb and flow. Future is my home, and I'd like to stop dreaming.

Written at the beginning of 2022, I was tired of both replaying memories to thrust me into what I no longer had and simultaneously tired of my head in the clouds. Earth to Christine! I needed to be present, but I wasn't sure how until I learned to experience God all around and in me. The more I surrendered to Him the ideas for my future and the memories of the past, the more peace of mind I had. I only recently realized that a sound mind goes hand in hand with being still. I thought being still was a physical surrender—and it can be. Having a still and sound mind is resting in the truth rather than filling in the blanks. It's a state of mind.

All the pockets of rest I found in the chaos were found by being mindful. The word *mindful* was like Lord Voldemort and I wasn't thinking of it nor doing it. I could find rest externally, and it would often temporarily quiet the loud inner voice, but it would come right back. I developed a love for nature from a young age, and I could experience God all around me, but I hadn't realized that I could allow Him to be Lord over my heart and mind. I didn't quite compute this from the inside-out healing. The external stuff—I had that down. The internal bits—ain't no way! The more time I yielded to the Lord, the more I naturally found peace. I no longer looked to external stimuli to find comfort, peace, or joy. I had found them from within, and they poured from inside to affect what was around me.

You don't have to run ahead of God to prepare your own way. You don't have to live with the sound of a broken record playing on repeat in your mind. You can be made alive to a new reality that isn't subjected to the past or the future.

It's the beginning of December 2023, and I'm adding clarity to this word from almost two years ago. God is right ON TIME—always. During yesterday's message at church, our pastor, Tommy Miller, spoke on this very thing. He selected three people to come up to the front of the church as an example of past self, present self, and future self. He elaborated on the idea that "time presents problems to our identity" while expanding that Jesus is the "I am." I *am* is the present tense. This present tense lives inside each of us and determines who we are. We are not defined by the past, our habits, or our future we believe is out of reach.

I am already the woman for the job. You are already the woman or man for the job. There is no striving you need to do to get there. You are. Jesus died for all and we co-died and co-resurrected so that we already are. Everything that was died. Miller said, "Nothing changes God." He further added that our behaviors are just "deeds" as with Colossians 3:1–11. We may need some time to shake off those deeds, but the behaviors don't define who we are. The behaviors are just habits that need reforming. When we take captive our thoughts (2 Corinthians 10:5) and we present ourselves as a living sacrifice as His church, His temple (1 Corinthians 3:16), those dead things are pulled from our growth. As a plant grows, the dead things are pruned off to ensure it doesn't affect the growth.

A Grieved Spirit

A GUST OF WIND BREAKS through a creaky window and bursts in like an uninvited guest. Its chill casts reckoning on the room where meaningless chatter once amused the walls and noise surrendered to its cause. Recalling raised fists in rage is futile in memory's old age. Rifts once made their way between, no longer invited to make a scene. Grievances are best left unsaid. When the light burns out, the end has come.

I used to believe that well enough was best left alone but lies covet truth on our lips. If not you, then who? If you don't speak, then who will? Sometimes we expect God in all His mysterious ways to physically reach down and take care of a situation, but God uses people. We are His doorways. If we do not walk a word out then how much do we believe it?

If you believe that He works all things together for your good, yet fear holds you looking at the past, how useful are you to the kingdom of God? Truly, I ask of you. Do you look like you believe His Word? Are you living in such a way that it looks like you've spent time with Jesus? This is not to condemn but to ask you for a moment to look in the mirror and tell yourself what you see.

Do you believe what He said to be true or are you still stirring thoughts that it's just not for you? Yeah, I've been there too many times to count, but I'm tired of feeling as if I'm the one left out. Surely, if He died for all, that includes me. Surely, the lies are not bigger than the victory! When reality looks like it is at war with what He says, we must stand on the truth. This is where faith is activated—against all certainty.

This passage above is a glimpse into the lies I believed—the lies I invite in to stay a while from time to time, but their only aim is to put out the lights. As I write this, I am doing it scared. All of it. I'm baring my heart to you, the reader, in hopes that the Holy Spirit speaks to you through the pains and learning that brought me to my knees.

Two days ago, my oldest son turned twelve. I don't know his

name or even where he is now. I used to be so consumed with the pain—his birthday would take ransom the rest of the month, sometimes the year and into the next, until something would break. I do this for him and for all my children.

What is it that we want to give them? We want to show them they are more than conquerors through Christ, right? We cannot do it by simply reading pages of a book. Do as I say and not as I do won't work, because it's not the truth. The truth is what we walk out. When we believe it, we act like it. I don't feel like writing tonight, and I don't feel like baring my heart to you or to God, but I will obey. We won't always feel like it, and sometimes that is the most powerful time to stand.

I believed for most of my life that it was better to be silent. Though I was often the loudest in the room, I didn't believe what I was saying was true, and the important bits remained silent. Now that I've seen Him show up and open doors that seemed like steel, I can't fake what I know to be real. Even in times like these, I know He is faithful to complete. Watch and you'll see. He makes all things beautiful in time.

Don't sit on your gifts. Don't stay silent about the things itching to crawl themselves out. There is wisdom in how we carry a message out, but we mustn't let the enemy win by living in a place of doubt. Sometimes another person's freedom looks like our opening our mouth.

If you were aware of a rapist loose on the streets, don't you think you would speak? Much of the time, the victims hide in shame and shadows, letting the villain fuel his insatiable hunger with more victims to feast on. What if you spoke up? What if you unleashed the very lie holding you in shame and helping another avoid pain?

Freedom for your grieved spirit is available, but it's found in your voice. "The righteous cry out, and the Lord hears, and delivers them out of all their troubles." (Psalm 34:17)

Grace Is Sufficient

"I FIND HOPE IN WHO you say I am. In you I am complete.
My future no longer looks bleak, now you are all I seek.
Hope surrounding my every day like sunshine breaking through.
All the love I have is because of you.
Grace comes crashing like a wave and settles on my heart,
For you I'd give my every breath, each day a brand new start.
You are peace. Your love it's always working.
I share in your joy even when I'm hurting.
God, your ways are higher than anything I know.
Lord, send me. I'll follow where you go.
I find hope in who you say I am. In you I am complete.
Hope surrounds my every day like sunshine breaking through.
And all the love I have, because of you."

His grace is sufficient. It covers all our sins.
If you find that are hiding, just let Him in
because the pain that's held you captive can be your victory.
Those moments of heartache are not the you He sees.
He is not a God that wavers or bends within the wind.
His love endures forever.
He longs to be your closest friend.
As easy as a knock or asking just the same,
He is there waiting for you to call upon His name.
His love is like a mighty wind that pulls you to your knees.
He is right and just, just listen to His authority.
For how can any man know what's written on another's heart,
but God knows each and every part.
With hairs that can't be numbered and a womb with mystery,
God knit us together and counted every hair you see.
His ways are always good.
Keep your eyes above the storm.
Lean in close and listen; nestle close to keep warm.
A moment can reshape history,

and with one small word, we have victory.
Speak the name of Jesus; let it reign within your heart.
He is longing for a relationship and to give you a new start.

Restoration

RESTORATION IS LESS SO ABOUT the prettied-up finished product and more about the process, the time, the grit, and the breaking down of layers to reveal the original beautiful form. It's about telling history and keeping intact all that's sacred and raw. Walls must come down, and often critters must be booted out. To restore is to return to one's original owner, the place we belong, or condition. The refining process brings out the most precious foundation.

The Promise

I KNOW IT'S COMING. EVERY day I wait feels like running turns to walking, and now I'm crawling on the floor, hopeless thoughts flooding through the doors of my mind. Rewind. I've fast-forwarded past the good parts. You were the God of my broken scars. I believed the lie that I have yet to live the parts of joy. The beauty exchange for ashes. I have not tasted untethered joy, and my heart leaps with anticipation at the filling of empty spaces. There is always more to draw from a well that doesn't run dry.

This journey is tough, and some days I don't want to get up, but Your spirit beckons me in the shallow and in the deep cries out to me. I know that You are within me always. You'll never forget me or a single tear shed in what was done at the hand of injustice. You wept and, for that, my hope is made strong. I know that You are faithful and what was taken will be returned, but until that day, in the in-between, I will consider how I wait. You get all my belly laughs and my ugly cries, you observe the way my mind finds the treasure of who You are in all things, hidden in plain sight. You say that joy comes in the morning, through the mourning, and I'll find it in the waiting. You're the God of plenty, my portion overflows. Even when I feel weak, You are stronger still.

Sometimes all the strength is in the small movements, the giving of the last to another when you have nothing to give. "But when you do a charitable deed, do not let your left hand know what your right hand is doing, that your charitable deed may be in secret; and your Father who sees in secret will Himself reward you openly." (Matthew 6: 3–4) The small movements are often overlooked, but the very thing set to be last will be that which is first. God looks at the contents of our heart, so then if our heart posture is hate, but yet we serve those around us from that place, recording and boasting in our well-doing, we have ignored this caution. Let us give from the abundance of our hearts as He asks us, not for attention or to be given back. Freely given to us, we freely give. We do not give for approval of man, nor of power or position, but we give because He first gave. We lay it all down to see another be made free just as we are.

I am reminded of Elijah and the widow. The widow had so little food left for her son and herself that she said they were set to eat what remained and die. Elijah called her to make him a small cake and then give herself and her son the remaining. She did so, Elijah spoke a word over the widow, and it came to pass.

"For thus says the Lord God of Isreal: 'The bin of flour shall not be used up, nor shall the jar of oil run dry, until the day of the Lord sends rain on the earth.' So she went away and did according to the word of Elijah; and she and he and her household ate for many days." (1 Kings 17: 14–15)

This word continues on, and her child is struck dead from sickness. The same prophet who spoke life to a barren kitchen spoke to her son and he was made alive.

Her small movements, her honoring the prophet with the little she had, was a small movement yielding a BIG reward. When we lose everything, what matters changes. The widow was not concerned with the promise nor with getting something back for her obedience to Elijah. In Matthew, we read, "He who receives a prophet in the name of a prophet shall receive a prophet's reward." (Matthew 10:41)

Before this Scripture, we see mention of receiving a person and what they carry. The previous verse states, "He who receives you receives Me, and he who receives Me receives Him who sent Me." (Matthew 10:40)

What seems small—believing on a word of hope set in the pages of this lively book and in things not yet seen but believing for them anyway despite the circumstances—is actually quite BIG. The widow believed in He who sent the prophet Elijah. Her act of obedience opened the door for a breakthrough as both she and her son ate plenty and her son's life was miraculously saved.

Life may look bleak, but may I contend that what you believe in the in-between matters? When it looks impossible, draw from the well of possible. "It looks like this"...but God says. "This happened before"...but God says. The world is flipped on its head when considering the kingdom of God. God qualifies the called. He does not call the qualified. He looks for openness, not perfection, so then He resists the proud and rests on the humble. If you are empty, you can be made full of Him. If you are full of yourself, you've got no room for Him. Impossible is where He does the possible. Light shines the brightest in the darkest of places. Every seed has an outer shell that must break to birth the plant.

What are your dark places?

_____

_____

_____

_____

_____

_____

_____

Is there anything God has asked you to do or give?

_____

_____

_____

_____

_____

_____

_____

_____

What are you doing in the in-between joy and mourning,
breaking and breakthrough?

_____

_____

_____

_____

_____

_____

_____

_____

Barren to Bursting

JUST LIKE A TEST IS for the testimony, consider the barren places in
your life. Those barren places are exactly where God wants to show
up. "Do not remember the former things, nor consider the things of
old. Behold, I will do a new thing, now it shall spring forth; shall
you not know it? I will even make a road in the wilderness and
rivers in the desert...to give drink to My people, My chosen. This
people I have formed for Myself; They shall declare My praise."
(Isaiah 43:18–21)

God loves BIG. He splits seas. He shows up in the fire so that
you may not be scorched by the flame. The flame nor the waters

will overtake you. God is holy, and He made you righteous so then your barren places must also be filled and reflect His heart. Righteous means "to be made right." He is just and righteous. He makes all things beautiful in His timing. The goal is that you are made righteous so that you reflect Him in all you do and say and in the ways you move. You look like who you spend time with, so then let His Word prune the dead stuff. Lay aside the things of old so that you may receive the living waters in those barren places. You must be emptied of self so He can come in with His living waters and revive what looks to be dead. Don't you know that Lazarus was only asleep? Wake up and perceive it.

What are the barren places in your life that don't look like God?

_____

_____

_____

_____

_____

_____

What does God say about those areas?

_____

_____

_____

_____

_____

Submit those areas to God. Speak His words over those barren places. His words are prophecy. Faith is hope in things not yet perceived. Speak. Declare. Stand on His Word when it looks impossible. God will part those seas in the face of your impossibility. God will do it. If you are full of yourself and your ways, how can you be filled by Him and His ways? Those barren places are the places where He shines best.

A New Song

MY HEART HAS LONGED FOR this day, with anticipation thinking I had years to wait. I found it inside to wake up from a deep sleep. The Spirit of God no longer allowed me to keep hold of the lies that left me paralyzed by fear. He is calling out His people, unfolding a new year. Song will break out to glorify His name. The magnitude of His glory, none other deserves the praise. All will see the oil pouring out where there was once a lack. No longer an ounce of doubt. We'll call out "Abba Father, to what do I owe?"

Abba Father's reply: "No price befits my heir. You are also seated at the throne. A modern-day Cinderella from cinders to grace. You've obeyed in the hardship and committed to seek my face. I'm calling hope to arise. Let every voice shout my praise. Your cup overflows for all of your days. Oh, heart of a giver, let this be your song. I'll love you forever. This is where you belong. My kingdom is within you wherever you go. Let fear be beneath you, and let your heart glow. New beginnings are coming. I'm restoring the lost. I'm no respecter of persons. I'll show them who's boss!"

Thought Takes Flight

THERE SHE SITS, PEERING OUT between lace curtains, chin resting on her hand as she brushes curls out of her eyelashes. Her eyes sparkle with a depth of concealed pain. Her smile is content, subtle, and not overly defined. She gazes at the birds as they flap their wings in a war with the wind, a dance for the enjoyment of flight. The tussle is for favor of the bird feeder shaped like a little church dressed in soft yellow. Her eyes wander as she considers the depth of this moment, waiting for the breakthrough but settled enough to enjoy each breath as her chest rises and falls. Her heart groans and hungers with anticipation. As the little feet pitter-patter on her porch, blue jays and cardinals, sparrows, a word comes into remembrance.

"Look at the birds of the air, for they neither sow nor reap nor gather into barns; yet your Heavenly Father feeds them. Are you not of more value than they?" (Matthew 6:26)

This word wells up in her spirit giving life to her lungs as she exhales thanking her breath, tending a heart that takes delight in the Word of the Lord. She sifts through memories in her mind, recalling His goodness. Yes, He is for her. He is Jehovah Jireh, the provider. Being more so attended to than a beast with thoughts and movement that transcend the impact of a bird, His provision stretches wide—beyond food and livelihood. They are sustenance, food and drink for the spirit, the soul, all the crevices that thirst, and every dry and aching land crying out for water.

She is enamored by His love for her and relishes in His Word as she examines the trees, their arms stretched wide and far above the pavement and light posts. They have stories to tell. They've long existed to cast shade for the weary and stand strong against the wind. Their branches are many, and their language unheard for they speak with an ancient hush we have not ears to hear. She takes in the song of a sparrow passing by and returns her gaze to the consideration of pressed toil.

Looks Like Love

WHEN I SMILE, LITTLE CROW'S-FEET rest at the corners of my eyes. Deep grooves act like parenthesis around my smile as if to say "Take notice of this joy." A simple beauty I've longed for, and now the mirror is not an enemy of mine. I call her friend because she gives me a glimpse of what's inside. My face reflects my heart, content with the posture of joy, the wrinkles that define where I've gone and where I'm going. I have a glow of oil, mourning to joy.

Each day, I flip on the light and look into the eyes that once took each step looking at the earth from where she'd come. Now, she stands with grace and dignity as she knows her name. Worthy calls for her, and she answers. Beauty settles in. She has made a home here with me.

The tears of yesterday have salted my cheeks, adding to the birthing of beauty. Ashes to ashes, dust to dust, I lay this old man. I must. She is beauty; she is grace. His goodness she does taste. I won't answer the call that shouts "Not enough." Love keeps no record of wrongs. He sees me as I am, and I return to Him, knowing this is true. He created in me something new.

Comfortable with Freedom

I DON'T WANT TO TUCK in the memories I have of you, turn out the lights, and let them rest in a forever slumber. There is comfort in hiding within the Christ-sized void, feeling nothing, numb and passing by the troubled waters named Pain. In these times, isolation whispers lies like she is somehow a warm blanket and the hum of quiet is friendship. Some days, the water rises and grips me like a monsoon with whipping winds driving the waves so that I seldom come up for air. I hold my breath, tongue pressed against the roof of my mouth, and shoulders clenched like balled-up fists, afraid I do not move. Your touch breaks the chaos and breathes life into the barren. You breathed life into me and designed me to weather this storm—to call to its waves "Be still!" This too shall pass. Peter, look at the son. When all else is dark and draws you into its waves, look up.

Be so comfortable with freedom that the sound of chains is dim, no longer calling you home. Give Him your ashes so that He can make beauty. Give your tears so that He might shower blessing on you with the jar of tears He never let hit stoney ground. In times like these, be still and know. He is God and we are not. Emotions are temporary. Testing is only to produce a testimony. Let that be enough. Take refuge in His safety.

More Than You Can Carry

GOD DIDN'T SAY HE WOULDN'T give you more than you could handle. He does. He gives it to you because you are not meant to carry the weight. "Take My yoke upon you..." (Matthew 11:29)

You are given things that will crush you, and that crushing will produce an oil. That oil is an anointing used as a testament to give God glory and show Him in everything you touch.

All the "impossibles" direct eyes to the God who is the only one BIG ENOUGH to handle it. Thinking you can do it alone will reduce who God is to the box you expect Him to move in rather than seeing His reverence and just HOW BIG He is. He is not your earthly mother or father, your sister or brother, the one who hurt you. That's not Him.

Sometimes things are our own doing and other times a product of our environment. It's not always our fault either. Testing produces a testimony, and you'll find that when those blinders are removed, you see with new eyes that God was always there. He sends blessings through people—a grade school teacher, a counselor during the divorce, a best friend you weren't allowed to hang with. He uses the things we know to speak to us until we fully know His voice. We can hear Him speak through the pages of the Word and through the things we know. And now we can see that it all aligns with the character we've gotten to know in His Word.

The Word does say that He will make a way of escape, however, and that no temptation will overcome you. (1 Corinthians 10:13) I believe that's the one so misquoted. He makes a way of escape, but when you don't know who you are and whose you are, you'll keep eating the counterfeit rather than the bread of life. You'll chase down the greasy burger rather than the steak salad—if you catch my drift.

The more time you spend with Him, the more you look like Him. You become what you surround yourself with, so then your heart looks like His. "You'll know them by their fruits." (Matthew 7:15–20) I'm not talking about behaviors. I'm talking fruits of the spirit that reveal heart posture. Gentleness, love, long-suffering.

(Galatians 5:2) Yeah, that last one. So many don't list that one. The irony. The crushing produces the fruits of the spirit quite naturally. You find out how to love when you've been stripped of it all. You find out what it means to have joy when you experience great mourning. The test produces the testimony.

God won't force Himself and, in fact, if you are full of yourself, how can He fill you? He CAN do all things, but the relationship is not at gunpoint. It's a choice. So then, in the dumping of self, the being made humble, the crushing, we can be filled. How easy is it to fill an empty cup versus one full of liquid with only a small amount of room?

"I'm good with that God as long as it goes like this..." That is you sitting on the throne or sharing the seat, giving Him a measly inch while He wants your whole heart. He is good. He is not like those who let you down. He wants to fill you up.

What are you holding onto that isn't allowing Him room to move and have His way? "Thy kingdom come, thy will be done." (Matthew 6:5–15) Not your will or mine. In fact, our way will land us flat on our bottoms again and again. How many years do you want to spend in the desert? The Israelites spent forty! Complaining and griping, looking back and preferring their suffering in bondage as slaves, they wasted forty years. God does restore time. He already knew you and chose you regardless of what you'd do or say. But, you have a part to play in faith.

Your obedience is an act reflecting your heart and what you believe in. What do you believe in? If God says to do something and you don't do it, it reveals that you don't trust Him in that area.

Give Him the reins. Aren't you tired of that same ditch? You keep looking in the rearview mirror, honey. There is nothing for you there other than a quick glance to recall the blessings of God and shift to a new lane, a new opportunity.

Don't wreck.

Let Jesus drive.

Let Him take the wheel.

What areas of your life are you still trying to take control of?

_____

_____

_____

_____

_____

_____

_____

_____

How can you practice letting go?

_____

_____

_____

_____

_____

_____

_____

_____

_____

_____

_____

PART THREE

ALL AROUND US

"Do not go where the path may lead.
Go instead where there is no pth and leave a trail."
— Ralph Waldo Emerson

God Speaks

WHEN GOD SPEAKS, ALL OF creation stops to listen. Their Creator's words are like honey.

You can find the certainty of the Holy Spirit in the flutter of a hummingbird's wings, moving swiftly but unseen. You know He is moving, but you don't know His moves.

The laughter of a monkey reminds us of His sense of humor. He tells us to be like a child, relishing in the nature of life and love.

The vast oceans of blue, desperately intriguing and begging to be discovered, remind us that He is mighty and a sight to behold as we sit reverently at the crash of a wave.

Each morning brings with it songs of birds reminding us that joy comes with the morning, a new opportunity to love as He loves, to do as He does.

The mountains in their height remind us to track paths not discovered for He goes before us behind us and all around us. He knows the way, and the mountains take a bow for the King of Kings.

The colors of the fall remind us that there is a season for joy, for mourning, and for everything in-between. Every chapter must end to bring with it a new beginning, laying to rest the former things.

His voice is a small hush found in the silence. We know Him by the time we spend as we listen, gently tending to the garden, elbow deep in dirt as the crickets beg us to come indoors. His voice is found in the crackle of a fire with the hum of nature's song all around. It's the stillness that drives an insatiable hunger to know more—more of who He is and all we are.

He speaks through everything. Are you listening?

The Circle of Life

THE CIRCLE OF LIFE WAS made to be a revival, laying old things behind to steward well the things to come. There is an anointing over *The Lion King* film to capture the heart of the Father. A humble king was hidden in protection until his time for release to be set above every tribe. He had to learn his voice, practicing his growl until one day all the earth shook as he roared in his God-given authority.

Every knee will bow and tongue shall confess that you are Lord. As he sits above all the tribes of gazelle, elephant, giraffe, and water buffalo, they bow to him. He has that of hinds feet, delicately ruling in authority, living between an oxymoron, stewarding authority while under another much greater than he, and careful to give words of instruction with wisdom, grace, and power.

His voice is heard through all the lands, and the fear is of reverence and honor. They look on him with expectation for what is to come as he decrees and all those under the sound of his voice obey. They know their rank in the food chain. Even the things set out to destroy him know their place is to serve him.

He is the Lion, the Great I Am. When He steps, groups move to the left and right parting to make way for His entrance. All of creation sings together to welcome this King of Kings and Lord of Lords. All glory is His. Ancestors cry out from the heavens having caught a glimpse of what had been foreknown. Jesus, the Messiah. Son of man. Make way! Make way!

Be Still & Know

A THICK, SMOKEY FOG HANGS over the evergreens like blankets of cloud, and the air leaves a bite on the skin, chilled and bewitching. Faint sounds of chirping and waves crashing envelop the air while the mysterious feels like it's caving in. What is a life with perpendiculars, safe and predictable? How much more are the wilds, chaotic and noisy, unknown and hidden? Crashing waves beckon a stillness from deep inside, breaking through the hum of busyness.

The Wild Is Chaos & Beauty

PERHAPS LIFE'S BEAUTY IS FOUND in the disarray, in the organic function of living to its fullest without restraint. Perhaps the waves teach us great wisdom as they crash and retreat without apology, living to breathe and kiss the sands. Being still comes with great distress for a child with an ache to go, a zeal to touch and feel newly discovered places and hidden gems. But stillness is where we learn to listen to what the trees dare to speak to us as their leaves rustle in the wind and foxes yip while deer graze, living life unashamed. Doing what they're made to do, why are we the few who stamp a seal of disapproval on our own cause? It's not enough.

Perhaps what we long for is to get lost in the noise, to fade into the chaotic bustling nature, and to be made one with creation, adding our own tune to a magnificent orchestra singing adoration for the Father of every fiber of this life. The fabrics are woven together in a pattern none can comprehend except the one who sees the final work. Perhaps you were born for such a time as this.

Brave Beauty

THE SUN'S BEAMS ARE BENT toward me while the sand buckles beneath my feet. My toes submit to thousands of grains, entangling my body with the earth. Waves kiss the dry sand gently and reliably. I've become weightless in this place, caressed by a beauty I cannot fathom nor understand, an escape of peace known by all of man. Here I find You calling out my spirit a place of sweet release, so as the breaking of waves and a whisp of the wind. Solace is here; danger is here. I'm reminded that I am just a small speck with a bright light as I leap into the deep unknown. Here I meet my fear and here I let it go.

Starving To Be Full

EACH OF US IS ON a journey of discovering our roots and what binds us to God. Whether we say we believe or not, our spirits groan for God. Someone hungry for nature, always hiking and seeking adventure, fills that place with God's creation. They could denounce God with their lips, but their spirit craves its Creator.

A painter finds the Creator.
A hiker finds the Creator.
An animal lover finds the Creator.
A writer finds the Creator.
We find Him in ALL things.

Kingdom Garden

WE ARE SEEDLINGS IN THE kingdom garden planted by our Father—each given a measure of faith. We toil in vain and give way to weeds that take over the tender sprouts we breathe. As our Gardener takes a knee to pull from the earth and we cry out to the Son, we are found in His marvelous grace—a little hunched over but not undone. Soon, we thrive with the daisies and face each day with gratitude. As our leaves and petals reach higher, we humbly recall from whence we came, but we don't stay there. The weeds are beneath our fall. Our Gardener is gentle and takes care of all. He keeps barriers to keep critters out. He tends to the soil, ensuring a rich investment. According to Isaiah 55:8, His ways are not our ways, and His thoughts are not our thoughts.

We are invited to both give and take from this overgrowth of garden, vast with wildflowers, fruits, vegetables, and varying leaves and colors. Each form is like tongues divided yet singing in one accord, all releasing seeds to multiply and strengthen the whole. We look around and observe nations of growth, cross-pollinating and always reaching new heights. One day, when we all wither away, as we all do, you'll lay the customs and prayers down as a foundation for future generations to reap a bountiful harvest boasting on ancestors of old—their words, their spirit, their history to be made tangible for tomorrow. We bless those who bud beneath.

Romans 12:3–8 references the body in its unique measure of faith, having a separate function, being one individually gifted. The written word speaks greatly on bearing fruit and seeds, harvesting, reaping, and sowing.

Go forth, wildflower. Stay wild. Do not worry for a thing.

Rising from Ashes

I AM FROM FIELDS OF green that stretch on for what looks like forever—the staple aged-red barns, pastures, and small-town "how ya doin's." But more than that, I am like a phoenix, rising from the ashes I was born into. I've heard it said that, if the previous generation doesn't carry the torch, it is passed to you. My life has looked like pain for as long as I can remember, and without pity and only the desire to grow, I've known it was purposeful.

The phoenix is an immortal, regenerative bird that rises from the ashes. Its strength to overcome boasts great courage. It worships the sun, and I believe it's the source of regeneration—beauty from ashes.

I am from the underbelly of shame, taking flight out of the loss of innocence, rejected by all but one. When you're beautiful, it seems like a gift, but it's another heaping pile of ash to know that you are not seen, you are not known, and you are certainly not heard.

But the Son, He is warm and inviting. His invitation never relents, and joy comes in the morning as He clothes what was dark with light. I come from bitter winters and freeing springs—from hardened earth crusted with strength to delicate flowers stretching their petals to catch a glimpse of the sun. This dichotomy is unstable; it begs often, feeling like an intruder, crushing my hopes, and testing my faith. I come back stronger.

Some verses act as the wind beneath my wings, and without them who would I be? "In my weakness you are strong." This could be an anthem for my life. "I can do all things through Christ who gives me strength." It's exhausting to be the strong one all the time, but my strength has never been my own. I look in the rearview for a glimpse only to recall the ashes I was born from. I return my gaze to the Son as I rise.

The more I learn to embrace my golden scarlet feathers, the more I learn to soar. I cannot do it in my own strength, but I can allow the wind to carry me, resting in His peace. While I come from what burns, leaving ashes all around, I know there's another in the fire, and He calls me to fly again.

"And He said to me, 'My grace is sufficient for you, for My strength is made perfect in weakness.' Therefore most gladly I will rather boast in my infirmities that the power of Christ may rest upon me." (2 Corinthians 12:9)

"I can do all things through Christ which strengtheneth me." (Philippians 4:13)

You Can't Change a Flower

"YOU CAN'T CHANGE A FLOWER" is a phrase uttered by my four-year-old son, Emerson. The wisdom that pours from his lips has me in awe sometimes. One time, I turned down the radio to hear the song coming from his heart. He sang, "Flower, flower, I love you." When I asked him about it, he said the flower was me.

A flower is as made—no matter the sun and no matter the rain. She can only grow, you know. The sun guides her to stand strong, and the rains give her drink. Nothing can change a flower's petals or her scent. She is unique with not one exactly like her.

You, friend, are a unique flower. No one is like you. No one can replicate your laugh, your smile, or your song. Don't fall into the trap of comparing your beauty to another. It's like comparing a

Picasso to a Rembrandt. Only the artist knows the value of what he has created—all of the nooks and crannies. God delicately sweeps His brush across the page as He forms the petals adorning you like the garments of royalty. He finds the most nimble brush to add the details. No one can copy His work. Your stem is sturdy, it's firmly rooted, and though no one else sees the work it took to stand tall, unable to observe the roots beneath the surface, He knows.

"Which of you by worrying can add one cubit to his stature? So why do you worry about clothing? Consider the lilies of the field, how they grow: they neither toil nor spin; and yet I say to you that even Solomon in all his glory was not arrayed like one of these." (Matthew 6: 27–29)

Where lilies are planted matters. They survive in full sun. Their stems are strong and tall, and their beauty is unmatched. Their bulbs need the right kind of soil. They are dressed in beauty, and they know how to take the show, but they don't look anywhere but the sun. Here, lilies are compared to Solomon's glory, yet they supersede Solomon. Solomon was a king—he was royalty. A flower is strong because of the nutrients it gathers in the depths of where it is planted (what is done in private) while roots form and stretch beneath the surface. A lily starts as a bulb and slowly springs up a green stem. Another term for the part connected to the stem of a daylily is a crown. Foliage dresses the lower parts of her kind, and eventually, the bud blooms in all its glory and reveals stunning petals and color. Without the sun and the roots, she would not stand.

"But you, when you pray, go into your room, and when you have shut your door, pray to your Father who is in the secret place; and your Father who sees in secret will reward you openly." (Matthew 6:6) The roots of a flower are the secret things no one knows about. No one knows the tears you shed, the songs you sing, the prayers you speak but God. He honors those roots.

"But the ones that fell on the good ground are those who, having heard the word with a noble and good heart, keep it and bear fruit with patience." (Luke 8:15) Seed must fall on good soil to produce a harvest. It must be tended to properly. When planting a lily bulb, you know you'll yield a lily. Every day, you will go and water her knowing that even if you don't see the roots taking form beneath the surface, she will grow. You lean on the understanding of sowing and reaping. Your patience and consistency birth what was in the seed.

Is there something God has given you in seed form that you are waiting to see manifest? How are you caring for that thing? If God gives you a seed (idea) to start a business, what are you doing with that seed? Are you praying over it (watering it)? Are you asking Him what to do with it or are you just hiding it under a bushel? Hiding your light is as simple as hoarding the very gifts, talents, and ideas God gave to you. The lie comes to kill that seed. Maybe you've heard whispers that you aren't good enough, it will fall apart, no one will believe you, or why bother because last time...

The good soil is "a noble and good heart" and one that is also patient. Prior to verse fifteen, we read Luke 8:13–14. Those who hear the Word but don't do anything with it still have the seed. It falls away or falls on thorns and is choked out due to taking the seed and running after our own desires rather than being submissive. In this case, the seed does not mature. Here's what James 1:23–24 says:

"For if anyone is a hearer of the word and not a doer, he is like a man observing his natural face in a mirror; for he observes himself, goes away, and immediately forgets what kind of man he was." Without applying faith, without faith tested, it's not really faith but a good idea. Our nature and character must reflect what we believe or we don't really believe it. If someone were to say "I'm a trustworthy, loving person," but yet their actions reflected someone who cheats and lies, it shows that his words do not match his actions. Therefore, we conclude that since his words flow from his heart (Matthew 12:34), his heart posture does not reveal him as someone that is trustworthy and loving. Our actions and words are a mirror of what we believe in our hearts. Reading on into James, we find more clarity:

"You see then that a man is justified by works, and not by faith only. Likewise, was not Rahab the harlot also justified by works when she received the messengers and sent them out another way?

For as the body without the spirit is dead, so faith without works is dead also." (James 2:24–26) Rahab hid the messengers and protected them. Her actions revealed her heart posture and what her faith was in. Think about Noah as well. If he had only heard the instruction of the Lord and did nothing about it to build the ark, he would reveal that his trust was not in the Lord. It would show that he didn't believe a flood was coming.

Let's be keen to listen and obey. If you believe Him and that He is good for you, then what He asks of you will produce something good. He is a good papa, a good friend, and a GOOD GOD. Be a doer of the Word to reveal what you have your faith in. Let your seed (your words and your beliefs) be watered by faithfulness (praying, acting, asking) so that it may spring up and reveal what is intended.

You, darling flower, were made for such a time as this, but you've got to obey what He is asking of you. A seed planted but not tended will die. You can't expect to heal the hidden places without giving them to God. You can't grow unless you are willing to put in the work by trusting it ALL to the Lord.

What you hunger for will be revealed in what you eat. Taste and see that He is good. You've got a seat at the table. Eat His Word. Live His Word. Nothing tastes like it. No love can compare to His. You are what you eat. You'll also taste the words you speak as they are released. Eat good things. Speak good things. You are a stunning lily. Act like you believe it.

What are you speaking? What are you believing?

_____

_____

_____

Is God asking you to do something as an act
of faith to birth that thing?

_____

_____

_____

Planted in Good Soil

GARDENS ARE A PLACE TO dig in the dirt, play, and discover what lies beneath, the roly-polies and the earthworms. We dig deep to gently lay in its home a new sprout with delicate leaves and hopes as big as the mountains. A sunflower starts off small but grows up to an average height of six feet tall!

We tend to the plant, and we water the earth. What we dig into will show on our hands. Our soil will reveal our foundation.

Are we moved by the wind to be uprooted each week when the storm comes? Are we planted in good soil, drinking the nutrients needed to thrive? Seasons come and go. They change. There is a time for joy, for mourning, for weeping, and for dancing.

May our roots run deep to a well that runs not dry. Our Gardener, He speaks to us. As we are just a sprout, He delicately soaks the soil around our feet, carefully using kid gloves as we move with the water. Like an infant on milk, we cannot yet digest more.

As the sunflower takes to the seasons, she weathers the storms, and she grows stronger. Her stalk takes on coarse hairs to protect her, like skin acts as a shield to organs. She grows through the winds. She stands firm and no longer sways with the wind but becomes like the wind. She stands firmly grounded, rooted in the right stuff. She started out as a cub and came up a lion. The Gardener grows pleased, and her face looks upon the sun. As long as she looks at the sun, her face does not droop. Proudly, she stands because she came from the earth, a little dainty at first.

Oh, the places you will go should you trust in the Sower. He takes the tears that you shed and makes it a shower. He pours blessing on the pains and turns the test into a story. All that has been birthed forms a beautiful testimony.

Who created the garden? The Gardener gets the glory. He knew what would birth from the seed.

Still in the Waves

IT'S IN THE STILLNESS THAT I find You are good—beyond the parallel structures that are well kept and defined—beyond the control of knowing what comes next. What is wild is Yours—no way to copy the yip of a fox or the petals kissed with morning dew. You are all that is. Your introduction is I am. The synergy that exists between our spirit and the great wide open dissolves lies that keep us confined. "Who are You" inevitably answers the question of "are You good?"

You are the wind taking leaves into flight, causing an enticing dance. You are the waters drenching the barren, the thirsty. You are not predicted, yet you are trusted. The oceans hold secrets in its deep underbelly, yet the invitation finds acceptance all the same. A beautiful dichotomy calls to us—wild and safe. What can be found is never lost but discovered in the evergreens and the stillness within her arms. Take your bare feet and loosen expectations as you run into the forest and where the wild things are. You were never meant to be kept.

Consider Wildflower

CONSIDER THE POINT OF VIEW of the wildflower, avoiding perfection in bushes and fields, growing among the weeds and flowers alike. To be without form, intricately designed within an ecosystem of great chaos, is natural. Freedom is in responding to the call of the wind, to what is wild. Why do we allow our hearts and minds to enslave us? Do we not govern our own? The Holy Spirit was once referred to as a "wild goose chase." What is wild remains free from the restraint of perfection. Flowers giggle and toil not, dancing in the wind and relishing in the sun.

The Rearview

OUR MEMORY CALLS TO REMEMBRANCE the goodness of the Lord. Written on our heart are words of life and breakthrough, images of laughter and dance, song and praise. A mind submitted to the Lord is clay, molded and redefined. Remember, don't you forget. Lay aside the cobwebs and darkness seeking to cloak the light.

I will remember You from the moment of my first heartbeat to the kicking feet from inside. The tiny fingers and eyelashes. The longing little girl inside of me who is beckoned to her Papa, never forgotten. Each tear collected is as rains of blessing and praise. I uphold His name on the sounds of my praise as I recall. Always remember.

The Earth remembers the creatures, big and small, as they are laid to rest, a foundation to feed generations to come. Our ancestors paved paths of old. History is alive in our blood. It's alive in the waters and in the soil. All of the earth groans for the Lord, singing and praising. The stars reverberate, the trees shake, and the waters roar. What the Lord is speaking in and through creation has no cap. Let not your mind forget. Let your lips continue His praise. Be given unto new eyes and new ears. For the day at hand calls for necessity what the things of old laid a path for.

Let the rearview be a glimpse of His goodness, peering into His faithfulness. The rearview is only used to transition into a new lane, a new opportunity.

Read Isaiah 43:18–21.

Breaking the Rules

WHAT IS A RULE? A rule is a set of principles governing conduct. Rules are meant to subject a group of people to behaviors that keep them in line—heading in the same direction. A million little feet sounding "left right left" propel movement to a confidential sound.

I've never been a fan of rules. I don't blindly follow the loudest voice, and I've had half a mind to oppose blind obedience since the age I sported a Shirley Temple head of locks. Wearing ruffles and curls, shades of reds on my lips, and delicate pearls with femininity and poise at its core, I questioned the seemingly opposing barefoot adventure. Torn between two worlds, I'd rather take the beaten path, find my way inside when the sun has fallen asleep and my feet pat footprints to show where I'd been.

Rules.

A dissonance, a little unruly, a little holy, exists beneath the balcony of trees, muddied floors, and the serene of the outdoors. Take me back to whence I came. From the chaos of branches and roots, leaves shaking with song, and rainy days that last too long.

Let us bask in the sounds of creation, and learn to sing like the birds or the hum of a bee. Let us kick off our shoes, run into the wide open spaces, and crawl through where no one dares turn. My bones ache with a longing to discover what remains unknown. How else do we discover how to be known but to know in return the place we call home? Jesus didn't exactly walk on the pavement. He came to set a new example, create a new covenant, and write His laws on our heart—not those of religious routine and no heart change. Ralph Waldo Emerson said it right, "Let us be silent, that we may hear the whisper of God." A transcendentalist writer, one who married nature to its Creator, God, understood the unison of a beaten path, a quieted mind, and He who made it all.

God was, for all intents and purposes, a rule breaker. While He did come to write laws on our heart so that, when in unity with Him, we may naturally have an internal compass to what is right and good, He also broke a LOT of rules set by the Pharisees. I like to think I'm a little like Jesus in this way. It reminds me of Merton's Strain Theory, a theory that broke down the understanding of defiant behavior. While Jesus was not necessarily defiant to the laws, He did write a new script giving a new perspective to the old one. Think of the disciples He used: Peter, Andrew, James, John, Phillip, Bartholomew, Matthew, Thomas, James, Simon, Thaddeus, and Judas. Consider the characteristics of these men and who they were pre-Jesus. Pre-Jesus, we are looking at murderers, adulterers, tax collectors, all the least of these—castaways of society. They were so broken that they could only be filled up. I guess my rule-breaking side feels seen by Jesus.

Let us swing wide the doors of our heart to lay to rest tradition and be open to His doing a new thing. Tradition is perpendicular. It is parallel. It is structure and routine, but the Holy Spirit was once referred to as "a wild goose chase." Take off your shoes, and let those toes breathe and explore. Think less of the mess and more of the mindfulness. Be present with who He is and His being in everything He created.

Transcending Thought

SOMETIMES, GOD, YOU ARE AS tangible as this tattered book. I can spend time diving into Your words and feast on the sustenance that fulfills every starving part of me. Being tangible has its limits. I can put You down when I want to slip into things of old. We both know I can't really do that—let You go. Just as You won't let me go. This bond is as blood brothers, connected by the tearing of flesh and blood, broken and connected.

Our covenant was written by the Ancient of Days. Your very breath was released into all things that take up space. You are not limited to this book. You are more tangible than the air or anything that can be contained. Your spirit goes with me dancing on the notes expelled from my lips—released into this realm to heal, to edify, and to break down lies. When my arms and legs break free of constraints or sitting in a rolling chair going nowhere fast, the sounds of chaotic joy lift my arms and press my legs to jump—to burst through the air. Alignment in the spirit. It marries what is physical to a personal being coexisting with me, for me, and I with Him. For I cannot part from Him nor He from me. Resist, if you would, the constraints of the pages. His ways were never our own. (Job 12:8; Matthew 6:25–34 ; Isaiah 55:8)

But if you will not bend, you will break. Does it make you uncomfortable these talks of spirits or realms unseen? Are you riddled with misunderstanding when confronted with His using the least of us to speak of wisdom? It's time to re-posture. Take a stretch or two and a few deep breaths. Take it all in. You'll bend. You won't choose to break. He is doing a new thing. Come along and see.

Pictures of You

SOMETIMES I FIND MYSELF SCROLLING into the past memories of laughter, movie nights, berry picking, family get-togethers, and tender moments. And I meet your eyes full of love so gentle and kind. I have this candid picture of you with your hand pressed gently on my pregnant belly, near time to meet your youngest sister, and your face is so delicate, your hand like feathers as your fingers graciously dance across my belly. You wanted to say hi too. I wish this photo brought me joy, but I can't help but study your sideways grin and wonder if you still experience joys like that—the intimacy of being raw with whomever you like whenever you like.

You did this thing where, out of the blue, you'd read me in a moment. As you passed by, you'd stop dead in your tracks, reach at my face, and caress gently with a stroke of your hand, testing my eyes, reminding me that I was beautiful or that I was doing a good job. Are you still sweet or has this heartache caused you bitterness?

If I could ask one thing, I'd ask you to remain open to pain because if you shut yourself off from it, that wall keeps out love, joy, and tender moments like these that I fondly reminisce.

The Giver of Life

WHEN I WRITE, IT MAKES me feel proud of all the places I've trekked and the person I've become. I expel all the pain from the deep under-belly of my heart, and my path for a vision is made clear again.

When I paint, I feel free to make mistakes and start again. It's the image of grace, add some time after, and erase. A splash of color and time gone by, you've got a mess of perfect imperfection.

When I dance, I am made one with the earth beneath my feet as rhythm and movement shake to the beat.

And when song falls off my lips, I am like the birds who sing just to praise their maker and lover, a song for all days. A note lifts higher than the pain that's buried inside and something folksy brings out the wild that's trying to hide.

But all of this exists to bring out the collection of art inside of us, a song, a movement, a vision, or a word to liven the spirit and shake what's been dormant for too long. We weren't made to stay silent but to sing a new song with hope on the horizon and all that follows is light. Watch the world set ablaze with joy as all of its people dance with change. Let us speak stories of triumph and leave defeat at the door. Let us empower one another and reach for more. Let us lead a new tomorrow for generations behind. Let us liven the gifts that have been dead inside. Lazarus, you have more life to live, so breathe in today and bid farewell to death.

Lost and Found

NOTHING LOST WILL BE LOST forever. Waves eventually roll back to reveal a colorful array of buried shells. A name once forgotten appears as a jolt at the top of our mind, suddenly and seemingly out of place. But nothing is out of place, is it? Just a detour to the final destination.

A dandelion blowing in the wind may disperse seeds on its journey, plant and multiply along the way. What is tethered to me cannot be too far away and will follow the connecting thread back. Like a child strung together by thoughts and emotions, cells and intentions. Once connected with a tangible lifeline, mother to child.

Just as no man can separate us from our Father's love nor can man separate a child from the Creator and doorway He entered. Every sheep is sought out by the Shepherd, no matter how far he wanders or how many holes the Shepherd must dig him out of.

Take Me Higher

SULTRY SOUNDS KISS THE LIPS of the one who speaks
"Thy kingdom come. Thy will be done."
My head is tilted back, sinking into soaring movements.
Higher.
Take me higher.
The droning sounds of hum fill the space around while we lift
and I sink into my seat,
pulling me into submission as my chest expands and retracts.
Possessed by the passion of being carried by the wind.
There is a wild beauty in soaring above it all in rest.
A quiet trust exists between the pilot and its passengers.
Serenity, release control, and be still.
The stillness fills this space
inviting a mindful presence of being known.
May I know you?
A stranger makes a shaky inch toward you
in an attempt to connect.
By shoes, hair, the book you're reading.
The solitude of letting go
and soaring is breathtaking in its commitment.
Gliding in and out of movements,
climbing an invisible staircase to the heavens.
Higher. Higher. I want to touch the moon.
I like the peace and quiet.
I'd rather connect to You.

PART FOUR

FRUSTRATED FORTRESS

"He is my refuge and my fortress
My God, in Him I will trust."
— Psalm 91:2

Bitter Roots

IF BITTERNESS IS A SEED, I've been sowing for far too long.
My knees have grown tired
and my tears have rained the crop.
If what I have to do is surrender to Your will,
I find myself desperate at the cost of this still.
Hours and tears have planted
this garden I've been tending for years.
I know it's not pretty all laden with thorns.
The weeds have taken over.
Imagine if it were yours.
Pulled up at the root, all bitterness and hate,
washed down with healing rain.
What is comfort in this place that I'm in?
I've grown used to the breaking—all alone in my sin.
My pain is a friendship or so I've told myself.
I've rejected the Gardener, refusing the help.
But if I plant a few roses,
nobody knows that the festering roots of despair
have taken control.
A war of roots, cut down all the same,
I want to be broken and given a new name.
Call me a giver of life like a mother of many.
I want to flourish like the daisies.
Let me grow like the lilies against every odd.
Let Your light shine upon me, roll out the new sod.
My garden is dying beneath what they see.
Help me, oh Lord, I want to be redeemed.

Mistaken

THERE YOUR SHOES SIT TARNISHED with mud. The last time they

held your feet you were exploring with your shoes sinking deep into puddles. I could try to put them on—try to retrace your steps, but the moments would be lost, for I could never force shoes on my feet that simply won't fit.

I felt your heartache and your pain, but every emotion was in vain. Women with insecure power delivered sentences without remorse nor shame—they too could not hear the desperate cries of your heart. Desperate to be heard in an adult world apart—is it possible that an anxious thought could become a foreseen memory?

I've held one painful moment that has plagued my mind like a tape rewinding back. Back. Back. Shrieks bellow from your heart like the foreign cry of whales calling their loved ones—shoulders drooped as a thought you knew released the signs of disapproval. Your body quivers and you yell with an anxious broken heart. "Mommy, where are you? Where have you been?"

That bitter desperate moment fades, and I filter through all the moments you may have considered this plea. You're angry in a schoolyard as kids pick and tease, leaving you isolated in your own fear, confusion, and rage.

A woman whose face is unknown tries in all her efforts to calm you down as you run out of the house in search of what you used to call home.

At night your heart calls to mine, and tears swell in my eyes as I swallow back the pain and conceal my ability to rescue you from yourself. We are not so different, you and I.

Outsiders try to treat the symptoms of the rage we feel inside. Your eyes melt with tears as deep and as painful as the ignorant adults who surround you. It's like you've been painted as a character who is stuck trying to peel back the layers to step out from behind—face doleful yet tempered with such intensity that you're mistaken for someone else. A case that would be too simplified to be referred to as mistaken identity.

I'll never fit in shoes that are not my own but I too share your effort in trying to peel back the layers of acrylic used to paint a character who resembles none of myself. You can't wear another's shoes, but you can always exchange yours for another pair. I love you, dear, and I'll love you no matter the shoes you choose to wear.

Fears like this became so loud that they enticed me into a soothing pain. I could fill in the blanks in my mind with what I feared was true mixed with some of what I knew to be true. This is a dangerous thing to do because the Word is clear about having a sound mind —"For God has not given us a spirit of fear, but of power and of love and of a sound mind." (2 Timothy 1:7)

A sound mind is stable, certain in understanding. It's like being still and knowing that God has this.

"Be still, and know that I am God; I will be exalted among the nations, I will be exalted in the earth!" (Psalm 46:10)

Allowing these thoughts to circumvent the very thing God tells us in His Word, filling the blanks with our fears, is foolish. How can we expect to move toward faith in things hoped for and not yet seen if we have imaginations we have created out of fear?

"For the weapons of our warfare are not carnal but mighty in God for pulling down strongholds, casting down arguments and every high thing that exalts itself against the knowledge of God, bringing every thought into captivity to the obedience of Christ, and being ready to punish all disobedience when your obedience if fulfilled." (2 Corinthians 10:4–6)

Those arguments are inside your mind. We cause invisible arguments to ensue within our minds, assuming and filling in the blanks of what could or should happen. The stronghold is by definition a fortress. A fortress is a wall built up for protection.

What walls have you built up to safeguard what is inside?

_____

_____

_____

The Word is clear about who our fortress is, and that is not us. We have to allow the Lord to bring our walls of self-reliance and self-preservation down so that He can heal those hidden places—so that we rely on His Word and His vision rather than our own. What does God say about it? Is this thought or image in my mind lining up with what He says and His character? Those are questions we must ask ourselves.

Ralph Waldo Emerson, the transcendentalist writer, whom my son is named after, said it best when he said, "The only person you are destined to become is the person you decide to be."

Your mind must be made up to know which direction to walk. Your mind directs your body which way to go, so make up your mind and be firm in it. Don't allow those thoughts an inch—a moment of your time to try and talk you out of your destiny or your destination.

"To be" is finite, so be it!

Like Arrows

I GRIEVE THE WOMAN I was, the Jericho walls that surround her heart. She didn't know the love of God, and her song to Him probably sounded of clanging cymbals. She could only extend what love she had to her children. How can one give a love they do not know? I knew the law. I understood behavior and earning, but grace was a far-off celebrity too famous for me to know, untouchable. These arrows, if left in my hands, could have ended up flying through the air without aim, but with the help of the Lord using all things, they will know the refined mother that their souls ache for. I found who I was when my tears hit my pillow, when the anger in me was too much to contain. I screamed out for help, and I thought You didn't hear me, but my God, You did. You knew the events that would follow and how they would be used to preserve our family, to heal the hidden places not touched by light.

My walls, all the lies I believed that kept me from love, had to be broken down. I thought that, if I did all the right things and kept my tongue from spilling pain, my life would look like yours. Boy, was I wrong. What behavior modification did was strengthen my walls. My walls became impenetrable until they weren't. It wasn't until an intervention came. Yes, an unjust one riddled with lies and accusations, but even that served a purpose greater than myself or my children. He works all things together for my good and according to His purpose. Yes, the crushing produced oil, the dumping of old wine, and the breaking down of the old wineskin for the new that brought revelation to my mind.

I didn't know love could taste so sweet. I didn't know it was for me. I held close the lie that I was the exception to love. After all, looking in my rearview, all I could see was replacement as a child, a mother, a wife. There wasn't an untouched area. But remember, testing produces a testimony. I needed to be refined. I hadn't understood the process so I believed that surely God is not good. I grieve this poor, helpless woman who ached for approval and who wanted nothing more than to be loved and seen by her husband, wanted and valued by her parents, and seen for who she really was. Time grew, and those walls became fortified by pain, shame, and selfishness.

I thank the crushing for breaking down the walls and for nearly seven years of breakdown to be brought back up. Dry bones came to life. My voice echoes love and determination, strength and grace. The old man, the grieved spirit, I lay her to rest. Her time has passed, and behold all things become new.

This piece was in response to a film I watched for a second time, probably three years apart, called *Like Arrows*. God is faithful, and He will use all things to serve His purpose. He knows all things, seeing all. He knows what you'll choose. He is aware of whether you'll obey and whether you'll disobey. Consider that in His timing He will make everything beautiful. If we would simply believe Him and His Word, what would things look like?

"He has made everything beautiful in its time." (Ecclesiastes 3:11) His promises are sure. It's a matter of whether we believe He is going to do it for us too. It shouldn't have taken the Israelites forty years. We can passively hear a word like that and think how ignorant they must have been—yet we do the same thing. The Word is not dated. It is just as applicable today as it ever was. It is a sort of manual to His people, so then why wouldn't it still be applied? Are we not His people? Did He not make us?

Trust Fall

SOMETHING IS SACRED ABOUT FALLING asleep on a flight experiencing turbulence or resting in a car no matter who the driver. Without having to be in the driver's seat and controlling the motion of your life, it allows for rest.

In Genesis, we are told that we have authority or dominion over all things that creep and crawl. When a dog is treated like a child, it produces anxiety because they are not meant to live with endless choices. Dogs are meant to be governed. Boundaries help a dog feel safe. In fact, when training a dog, keeping smaller quarters can help alleviate anxiety as they are getting used to feeling safe at home and learning to potty train.

To whom much is given, much is expected. When you can be trusted with little, God will increase your territory as He knows you will steward well what you've been given. We are like dogs in this comparison. We are governed by the Spirit of God. Contrary to what the world tells us, control is not the way to handle anxiety. The kingdom of God flips this world and its ideals on its head. You deal with fear and anxiety by relinquishing control to the One who can.

Take the chaos of a situation—rest looks like laying back and knowing that no matter the outcome, He has your best interest. When you feel safe, your chest cavity rests, your heart and breathing slow, and your body doesn't produce that nasty stress sensor called cortisol. We were created for rest, to soar as the Bible instructs. Soaring is the act of being lifted by the wind. No flapping and energy are needed. You just go where the wind takes you, trusting its strength and direction.

We trust the pilot because he has been trained to operate the plane. We rest. We trust the driver—well, sometimes unless they enjoy hitting curbs for sport—because they've passed a test. A double-minded man is unstable in all he does because he tries to put on his daddy's shoes, and he ends up tripping over his own feet doing it his way rather than submitting to God's way.

Far greater, we must lean on the Lord as He knows all things and He created the world and all the people in it. No matter the situation, He will see us through. He is for you, friend. He sees you. He knows your heart because He created it. Nothing is separate from the Lord. So go ahead, close your eyes, recline your seat, and buckle up for the ride of your life!

Preserving Love

I'VE ONCE HEARD IT SAID, "What is grief except preserving love?"

Yes, there is a time for grieving and mourning, but there is also a time for joy and laughter. We consider the oil of joy as an exchange for mourning. You must be dumped of self to be filled with the Lord. There is a time to release what you can no longer carry. If your hands are full of pain, how do you receive the gift of life? Tears feel like they are falling into an empty space, but we understand that celebration is the great underbelly of love. What is a marriage? What is a funeral?

Being connected with those in Zambia, Africa, I see laughter, joy, and celebration as they give their loved ones back to their Maker. Here in the United States, however, many of our funerals are adorned in black, mourning that overstays its welcome and a cloud of thick darkness that seems to follow one after losing what they believed was theirs.

Understanding that any connection first belongs to the Lord, having the right foundation, when we lose a friend, family member, husband, wife, or child, we know that with our release there is a catching of their Father. They belong to the one who made them first. We cannot stake a claim on someone beyond the Lord.

Yes, mourn their departure from this life, from your everyday experience, but even death is a transition into eternal Eden, a place of pleasure and delight, without having to navigate the throws of this world. Goodbye for now, but I'll see you soon. We will find one another again in our Father's house, a place with an abundance of room.

The Lord calls us to give to Him what is too heavy for us to carry. In our weakness, He is made strong. You don't have to carry it all, and like a husband, our Father wants to know that He is useful. He wants you to call upon Him to bear the weight. He knows that if you are full of yourself you can't be full of Him. Full of yourself is anything that seeks to boast itself over Jesus and everything He paid for. His blood was not in vain. When He ripped the veil, it gave you perfect union with Him. We died to ourselves as He too was laid to rest, and with so much focus on the blood here in US churches especially, we tuck away the resurrection. The resurrection was NO SMALL thing. He defeated the grave and laid to rest anything that sought to defeat Him or the kingdom of God and all its intentions. Process the pain, the rejection, the guilt, but don't let it be a cloak of shame telling you something is deficient in you.

He died for all. He paid for all, didn't He? The truth will set you free, so then what lie seeks to rob you of the life Jesus paid for? If truth sets you free and the opposing force has always been the lie, traced back to the Garden of Eden, then why are you holding on to something except the gift He freely gives you? You cannot pay for a gift freely given. You cannot earn or strive enough. All you can do is come to Him with open hands fully emptied of the old grave so that you may receive all He has for you. Do you believe Him? Act like it.

Do you think Noah believed in reality or what He heard from the Lord? Faith is hope in things not yet seen. It sure didn't look like a flood was coming. No one talked about great waters coming. He listened intently and gained detailed dimensions for a boat needed to refute the great flood coming for the rest of the world. Have you even considered what God says about a matter? You purchase a new piece of equipment, and with wisdom, you draw upon the instructions written by the maker so that you know how to operate it. Who made you?

Being still is profound. It's no wonder the Lord says, "Be still and know." His voice is small and still. How are you going to hear Him if you are always surrounded by other voices, by chaos? How do you recognize the voice of someone you don't know? How do you know someone without getting to know them—without spending uninterrupted time with them? When you spend time with Him, His voice becomes more recognizable, you desire more as you fall in love with Him, and then you trust His character. Now, you have staked a claim on His Word. When He speaks, you listen. You know He is good, so then you want what He has.

Little ears, what have you been listening to? What does God say about it? Has pain become a blanket you find familiar comfort in, unwilling to take a step, leap, or try? Pain means anguish and toil. Does He not ask us to let Him carry it? His name is one of perfect peace. Don't let a guest overstay his welcome. Satan is a salesman, and he is a good one at that. Would you allow a salesman to come in and offer him free room and food? I'd think not. What about a robber? Why do you have locks on your doors? It is to protect what is inside. Guard your heart. Emotions are temporary. You cannot live there. "Above all else, guard your heart, for everything you do flows from it." (Proverbs 4:23 NIV)

Are you looking through a broken lens or maybe rose-colored glasses? When your emotions are your guide, suddenly you are drowning in emotions only meant to be a stop, not the destination. Who made your heart and your mind? Ask the Maker to know how you work. You are His workmanship. This does require you to face the emotion, the experience, or mountain as well. Tucking it away and acting like you've got it together is just as dangerous. Not giving it to God is pulling up your bootstraps and deciding you got this because we can do anything. If He is made strong in our weakness, we have to expose our heart to Him to touch it. Any emotion tempts us to drown in it or hide it away. Neither is the healthy way to deal with it. Trying to be strong constantly is like playing God and drowning as we give it too much power. Letting the emotion stay for a meal, converse with, and uncover why it is there is stewarding your emotion well. Don't stay there too long. The deep wounds need a special touch. A festering wound too large for a bandage will become a sickness without being dealt with. Those wounds, those that seek to blot out our identity, those that may have been identified as PTSD or trauma, those need special care. You don't send a victim losing tons of blood to sit in a waiting room at the family doctor just like you don't go to the emergency room for a splinter. Healing is necessary. If you don't get those broken pieces mended, you'll take those pieces everywhere with you like Edward Scissorhands, and suddenly you're cutting everyone in your path. Are you harboring a pain that requires special care or are you treating a splinter like an ER visit—which is it?

We are given emotions to experience life. "I'm feeling angry or offended." Why? Those "negative" emotions are there to teach, guide, and act as a check engine light. Is it wise to look at another car and blame it for your car's check engine light? Of course not! Stay in your lane, and let God look under your hood. God made cars (people)—all types—and understands how we are made. Advice is great, but wise counsel is desperately needed when digging through the deep trenches of your mind. A military man home from a deployment in the Middle East battles different demons in his mind than a business man with day-to-day hardships. The warrior has to see a specialist who can relate.

Just the same, not everyone gets you, but God does. He created you and wrote the manual. You wouldn't go to a mechanic to perform heart surgery. And you wouldn't trust someone who doesn't know how to use scissors to style your hair. Go to the One who knows you. Ask your Father. Create the space to know Him. Let all the other voices be silent so you can hear Him. He desires you to be well. Do you want to be well?

Settling in

I DON'T KNOW WHAT IT means to not settle. All my life I've settled for an imitation, and I guess the taste grew on me. Impulsivity and pain were my dearest friends, and I'd jump at the chance to break my heart. Isn't that what it is when you chance the very thing you know will cause you pain? After all, the best friendships seep into your veins.

For the first time, I am longing for something pure, unbreakable, delicate, and generous. I feel a release in the need to bolster my own strength in keeping the pieces all together. Attempts at papermâché have become tiresome and childish.

To settle is to tuck away the hidden places, no longer allowing them a flicker of light to air out and breathe. It's finding contentment in the mundane, dreary air, despondent. But resolve is bursting from within, dreams of joy bubbling from my chest, twirling in the kitchen bellowing songs of purpose and of strength, a fist full of flour tossed in giggling whim and twinkling lights all aglow. Determined to put to rest the light inside, I will not do, committed to discovering the narrow path to find a man who sets my heart ablaze as You do.

Hidden by Shame

I SPENT A LIFETIME BEING replaced with women. I felt ashamed in my shoes to be gracefully undone—is there such a thing? But what I would give to look like that and take back all my power—sensuality—to keep him there. False love, relation-sinking-ship—counterfeit. Don't want your pieces. I'm hungry for more to be known and seen. See, I know my Creator, but honestly, I've been told that He made something broken, keeps me stored in the back with the cracked vases—can't see faces. Why me? Why have I been replaced—any chance to have more while being told to be less. I can't make sense of this nonsense!

I thought beauty was for the creator. I'm not a now and later. Enjoy me forever. I'm a Gobstopper that never loses flavor. I'm so tired of being stuck in space, out of place, never quite what you wanted. You said you wanted long legs and spray tans, so I obliged. Watch your eyes wander every way but mine. I'm just fine! Leave me alone, but please don't go.

This war inside is shame. I'm tired of hiding. What am I hiding for? I'm too much, so then go find less. Want someone slim with big breasts—choose the pole or walk down the aisle, but I'm not choosing you as my lifestyle. You're like a sinking ship, and I'll relinquish my grip just like Rose and Jack. Goodbye to all your good-time, empty lies. Goodbye to the shameful girl—it's time to come out of hiding!

Bandaids

I DON'T WANT A QUICK fix. I don't want to run away from Your Word.

This pain hurts, but Father, you've known. You've always known.

I try anything just to bandage this wound I've been carrying—like somehow it will just go away—dissipate—forget the pain.

I don't need to see a physician—I got this—under control—my control—lost control. Now what? So what.

Build a wall ten feet high. Won't let You inside. It's dangerous all these walls I'm facing—refusing to see my own reflection, it's tainted.

But why am I running and hiding from You—You are truth. The truth will set me free. Oh, I believe—help me in my unbelief. You say, do you want to be free?

Not me. No way. That would require change. That would require a shift. Address this need for control—it's endless. Bandaged, undone. Who am I when I can't run?

I don't want a quick fix. I don't want to run away from Your Word.

This pain hurts, but Father, you've known. You've always known.

Master Builder

AT TIMES I'VE REFUSED TO mourn, to face the depths of being in need, like a wall thick as those surrounding Jericho. I've become a master builder.

If morning came and I couldn't deal, I must have been weak. Let me be the first to say I'm in need, but in the quiet spaces, I fill them with noise, busy hands, and no sight of my void.

Without room to hear, I become deaf to any words worth hearing.

I traded the hum of a lazy Saturday for a day-long binge to simply create a space of constant noise.

I sold my peace for counterfeits that I could paint to look the same. My masterwork is a great showman battling the security of my pride.

If she were hurt, there were no more friendly conversations with reality. Each moon settles to invite a new morning, and all we can do is rest for a new day.

This girl needed her walls to be wrecked. Self-preservation will get you nowhere. If you build walls to protect your own heart and buy into the lie that was most prevalent in its genesis in the early 2000s—"Girl Power" and "You can do it"—you will not only fall but, behind the walls you built, no one will hear your cries. You locked yourself behind walls and refused anyone entrance. "You can do it" couldn't be a bigger lie. You need the Lord and His strength because I can promise you from personal experience if you are taking all your pain and trauma and carrying it on your back, you will eventually fold under the weight. This life is too much. God does give us more than we can handle, but He makes a way of escape and that way is Jesus.

I had such pride in my walls. They were fortified. No one was getting in, but more importantly, I couldn't get out. I was stuck with no one to hear me because I liked it that way. I definitely didn't need the help of the very people who abandoned me. Sound familiar? Just because it happened like this before doesn't mean it will again. We cannot lean on our own understanding or our own imaginations of what could or should happen. We certainly should not look to the past to get to the future.

Lay down those bags. Aren't they rather heavy? You don't have to be the strong one. Jesus took the weight for us. Your portion is resting and walking in who God says you are. You won't get a trophy for how much you've endured. No one is going to pat you on the back for your building skills, but you bring a great deal of honor to God with a life laid down where all the tests become testimonies. Let Him refract off all your broken pieces. He will mend those, and you'll become a lighthouse to others.

Hidden Like Treasure

You ARE HIDDEN LIKE THE ruby you are. More precious than diamonds and pearls, you shine. Pirates seek to steal your worth, so I've hidden you deep within my sands, warm and tucked away, resting and awaiting to be dug up by a man who will rejoice at his finding. He will show all what he's found. You will be seen; you will shine.

Do not be discouraged. It's time that you also know your worth. Don't sell yourself for a penny. Don't let the careless trifle with what they know nothing of.

You are priceless, a rare and unique find. Trust me, I made you. I assigned your worth, and there isn't one. You were carved from the very shine of the sun. None can compare to what I've made within you and what I've made you for. The man who is for you has been searching for you, and I'll uncover you when the time is right to reveal you when you are shining bright.

Ask How

"HAVING ACCESS TO SOMEONE MORE intelligent than you is a

blessing, not a threat." (Unknown) For as long as I can recall, I've wanted to be known for something other than my looks. I rocked my own style through the snide remarks.

"You look like a Barbie."

"Why do you dress like that?"

"You are living in the wrong decade."

This was too short, and that hugged too tight.

No matter if another wore the same, it would be pointed out and torn apart on me. This led to a constant obsession with perfecting my look. It wasn't an external expression of approval but an internal one. When comments or criticism came for the way I looked, I internalized a sense of lack and my only value came from the appearance everyone saw, whether appreciating or depreciating the value. Maybe I didn't let them in to see other things, but surely they heard my voice, the way I loved others, and noticed my writing and artistic knack from a small age.

My identity faded into the background of my father's life as he took center stage (though he was never truly seen and neither were his offspring). I would speak only to be heard, and when I was listening, I would often have my response ready to aim and fire at ready. I think I can speak for all of my siblings by saying at some point we felt like the stain on our family—not celebrated, just tolerated. What was birthed from this ache to be seen, not physically, but emotionally and intellectually, were roots of sexual distortion and attention-seeking behaviors.

I sought the arms of men who reiterated my feeling of being unworthy and unwanted rather than filling the void with something that remained. Unchanged. I was always changing. I ached for stability but had none. What was stable became a threat. What had wisdom was a threat. Anything that I felt I lacked became a threat. Intelligence. Passion. Expression through art. It was all a threat.

In my weakness, I am made strong, and for this, I have hope. If I have not, God has. I'm learning that there is grace upon sitting under those seated ahead. When you honor those before you, you walk into what they have. If a parent finishes college and provides a good life for his children, it is because he put in the dedication to attain his goal. His children greatly benefit too, eating the fruits of his labor. While I wait for the next step, I look at the footprints in front of me. I see only one set, and I've learned that my surrender has carried me a long way.

We don't have to have all the answers (and we won't). When you are thrust into being the strong one or the therapist among your friends and family, you lie to yourself. You assume you must have all because others come to you for answers. Wise humility learns from those who have trekked paths you have not. It is continuously learning about a thing—even if you think you've mastered it. It is to remain as clay, moldable, and teachable. What a simple solution it is to ask how, but for those of us who have been heavily relied on, it is like unlocking the mystery of a sound mind.

Ask how.

Heart Posture

EVERYTHING WE DO IS A reflection of our heart's posture. Maybe you aren't falling into the same trap because you are unclean, unworthy, or messed up. Maybe it's because you don't believe that God has better for you and that you are better. There are hidden places no man can know but God, and these places are revealed in our thoughts and speech. Traces of what we put our faith in show up—faith in old habits what we have always known and what's comfortable, faith in what's broken since we don't deserve to be whole, faith in never being enough and chasing what we'll never earn. That's why God instructs us time and again to think on good things and of good report—as a man thinks, so he is. Faith comes through hearing and hearing by the Word of God because He is the only one with the authority to determine our worth as our Creator.

We must know what He says above what our thoughts or others say. Our scope is limited. We build faith in what we listen to, our thoughts, what others say to or about us, lyrics in a song, or the show we are binging. We could look at our hands as if we are a farmer sowing seeds wherever we go and whatever we do. Those seeds of faith or doubt take root and blossom wherever we continue to come back and water. If we want to see an unhealthy habit die that has been sewn, watered, and tended to, we have to stop feeding it, caring for it, and let it die.

Ask God to reveal your heart posture and areas that you've been tending to that you need to walk away from and give to God. Likewise, if you want to see something flourish, believe for the outcome. The Word says that we have not because we ask not and if we ask in His name it will be given to us and our joy will be full. Seek. Knock. Ask again. Be persistent. Did God hear you ask the first time? Yes. But, we also find God when we seek Him with our whole hearts. He knows when we are including Him simply for a result and whether our hearts hunger for more in a relationship. Don't do better. Do different.

New keys for new doors. The same key won't open every door.

Running on E

SATAN HAS NO REAL POWER. He was already defeated. He can whisper, but we decide whether we run with it or combat it with the truth. We can resist him or let the idea (the distraction) take us for a ride.

In painful places, building walls and protecting the heart is easy. Sit in pain for far too long, and before you know it, you are asking how you got there. We are our worst enemies as we let an idea be like bait and take us for a ride as we are reeled into a whole other lifestyle and commitment. The distraction comes, and we must question why it seems appetizing. What is it seeking to fill in our lives? Why is that area not an area we are giving to God?

When we don't feel like we hear God in the chaos or stillness, what do we do and say? Do we stand firm on faith or waver? The test of faith is whether we remain hungry and fulfill ourselves with the Lord when in the hard times. We can find out a lot about someone by how they manage stress, how they treat their "enemies," and ultimately what their vices are.

Have you ever driven back roads or a highway with miles of farmland? What happens when you don't fill back up at the halfway point on the meter? You end up praying to God that somehow and somewhere a gas station will show up. Let's look at our lives like a spiritual gas tank. If we start to feel a little drained, we need to ask ourselves to take note and fill back up. We cannot run on E. We will end up stranded in a place we don't recognize.

Take inventory now so you don't wait until you are on E and stranded asking God to fill you back up. He will, but you will have endurance by continuing to fill up when you pay attention to your tanks.

Playing

SEE, YOU'RE PLAYING WITH MY mind again,
have me trippin' on my sin again.
Take my focus, take my drive,
leave me broken wonderin' why.
I'm at the door but I won't knock.
You've given me a stage, and I don't talk.
With vision in mind and truth in my story,
I want to surrender and give You the glory.
But these battles, they're unseen.
Make me feel dirty, though you call me clean.
See, sometimes I lie awake replaying all my mistakes.
God, I can't win. I can't win. Until I call on you again.

PART FIVE

TRAUMA & TRIUMPH

Fear is a hall of mirrors—our reflection distortion.
Jesus is the mirror of faith.

Tears for Tomorrow

I LAY MY SON EMERSON down for bed tonight, and I nestle into the couch. Some time passes, and I hear a cry for "Mommy!" I've always found the cry for Mama to be heart-wrenching, especially when it is a scared cry. I kneel down beside his tiny toddler bed and caress his blond baby hairs all around his face, memorizing all the lines. His eyes gaze and leave me, gaze and leave me once more. He was holding on to stay awake like he did as a baby wrapped in my arms, fighting sleep for just one more minute.

As I lay there with Emerson, I allowed God the vulnerability of looking into the painful places concerning my children. I could hear the cries of each of my children with that gut-wrenching cry for "Mommy!" My stomach buckled. I was in the broken spaces, and I felt the urge to pray for deep healing in each one of my babies. During that time when they felt like their mama had left their side and abandoned them, I felt that too. I would cry out to God in pain and anger, lashing out my disapproval for allowing such hatred to happen to my family and to my babies. I felt so alone, but even though I cursed Him in breaths, I spent others weeping for intervention and peace, justice, and His power.

I know that He will bring peace to each of my babies' hearts, and He will use their stories to glorify Himself. In that hope, I found peace, knowing that another family, child, woman, or man could be impacted, understood, and put at peace for even just one moment. All of our pain would be worth it. We serve a big God whose timeline does not reflect our own, and even when we don't see Him working things for good on our behalf, He is.

Just as with the wings of a hummingbird, the Holy Spirit moves. The movements of this bird are so fast we hardly perceive the wings at all. God is moving, always. We may not see it, but we hope in what is not yet seen.

I Forgive You

I FORGIVE YOU FOR THE shots you took at me, for the empty casings all around lying at my feet.

I forgive you for the victims you saw within my eyes—the little boy inside who once felt so alive.

I forgive the way you looked through me like pretty stained glass—it didn't last.

I forgive the way you held me close to shoulder the pain you knew I was too weak to carry.

I forgive the way you made me like your mother to keep your tears and hold back your fears.

I forgive you for the pain you caused—the way I dodged mirrors like a stain—something to hide holding nothing but shame.

I forgive your appetite for what wasn't yours—the way you touched me that aches through my pores.

I forgive the night you crept out of bed to steal kisses and feed the demons in your head.

I forgive the heart-wrenching pain that ached through my bones as my mind played games.

Not enough! Never enough! You can be replaced.

I forgive the empty I love you's and the vows that you made in vain.

I forgive the insults and the rationing of my sanity, every word that left me slain.

I forgive the man I knew. That's not your true name.

I forgive you. I could only imagine the life you lived and don't envy a mile in your shoes.

So for this, I say goodbye to every heartache and every cry, every repeated offense of men who I let undress every sensual part of me, condemning what kept me from being free. Goodbye to the nights when I fought for your love. If I said all the right things, then I'd be enough. Goodbye to acting the part, becoming a doll and a hardened heart. Goodbye past, you've long gone, no need to look in the rearview. I can't let this go on. A new horizon meets my gaze. For that, so long yesterday.

Let's Get Real

WHAT SUCKS ABOUT TRAUMA IS its insatiable hunger pressing us to yield to the weight of nothing and everything. Succumbing to a pit of nothingness and avoidance can be easier than it is to try and put my heart out there and trust that it won't be abandoned, crushed, or broken. Yet when I do allow myself the space to try, I find myself attracted to the same pain I'm desperately dying to avoid. A vicious cycle has healing looking like a mirage in this desolate place. I don't need all the pieces to fit just right. I want my lens to no longer be covered in a cloud—so desperate, these shouts of isolation are loud!

Why do I do the things I don't want to do? Paul speaks of such truth. Am I double-minded soaking in the sun atop the water and wrestling with the waves on other days? Yes. "For what am I doing, I do not understand. for what I will to do, that I do not practice; but what I hate, that I do." (Romans 7:15)

To heal requires looking at the hard things. It requires honesty and vulnerability. How is the doctor going to look at your wound if you are too busy covering it up? He won't. We go through things that are not fair, and this life does not promise days of no suffering. What we do with the suffering is what matters. Do we sit in the pain allowing it to eat us alive or do we get up and try again? To love, we must open up. We cannot receive love nor give it by keeping walls around our heart.

The first paragraph in this chapter is a lie I believed. I kept attracting the very thing I feared because I refused to look at who I'd become. I attracted the same broken people thinking I had it all mapped out. What pride I had in my pain—like somehow I deserved a trophy for all the trauma I'd endured. I found those same people everywhere I went—those who were comforted by the familiar and made their beds with the very demons they wanted to leave.

Healing is not a mirage. It is tangible, but God will take you back to the very thing that you fear the most to conquer it. What is fear but the absence of faith? If you are made to be more than a conqueror and you can do all things through Christ who gives you strength…if you are a joint heir to His throne and He has given you a new name, then what power does that fear have against faith?

"Yet in all these things we are more than conquerors through Him who loved us." (Romans 8:37)

"I can do all things through Christ who strengthens me." (Philippians 4:13)

"Even to them I will give in My house and within My walls a place and a name better than that of sons and daughters; I will give them an everlasting name that shall not be cut off." (Isaiah 56:5)

What is the place you fear the most? Is there something you keep guarded against everything? Maybe it is something no one knows about or only a select few know, something that replays in your mind, something that has brought a great deal of shame—write it down.

_____

_____

_____

_____

_____

_____

_____

Let us not be double-minded, but let us put on the mind of Christ, renewing our thoughts with His for us and for others. What does He say?

"But let him ask in faith, with no doubting, for he who doubts is like a wave of the sea driven and tossed by the wind. For let not that man suppose that he will receive anything from the Lord; he is a double-minded man, unstable in all his ways." (James 1:6–8)

"And do not be conformed to this world, but be transformed by the renewing of your mind, that you may prove what is that good and acceptable and perfect will of God." (Romans 12:2)

You'll begin to look like what you believe. He wants all of you—the good, the bad, and the ugly. You don't have to pretend with Him or put on a mask. Why not keep it real with the one who made you?

He already knows, so be real. If you've found yourself being hurt again and again in certain areas, I'd challenge you to think about what in you attracts that pain. I'd ask you to hide your heart in the Lord—to search for yourself in Him—to spend time in His presence and be renewed, restored, and revitalized. Healing is possible. Unless you allow Him to remove your rose-colored glasses or broken glasses, whatever lens you are looking through, you'll keep attracting the very thing that hurt you—looking to what is familiar rather than what He has for you.

"Do not remember the former things, nor consider the things of old. Behold, I will do a new thing, now it shall spring forth; shall you not know it? I will even make a road in the wilderness and rivers in the desert." (Isaiah 43:18–19)

Trauma bonding is real. You bond yourself to what is familiar and comfortable—even if it is harmful. When you get the healing you need, your desires change. You desire what He desires. Your vision and hearing changes. You see the heart, not the byproducts. You see the truth, not the potential. Potential is great. And potential is possible, but just like prophecy, it will fail. Prophecy can come to pass given the right circumstances—the right pairing with the Word. Just because it has been said doesn't mean the receiver believes it or acts on it. Looking with His eyes is so insightful because it is wisdom. Allow yourself time to heal so that you don't cut anyone on your broken pieces or attract the very thing you're familiar with in your pain.

"Love never fails. But whether there are prophecies, they will fail; whether there are tongues, they will cease; whether there is knowledge, it will vanish away." (1 Corinthians 13:8)

Love Bombing

MY EYES ARE DRAWN TO movement, to action—likewise is my heart. I see the parade of greenery as a dance not for display but for unity. Passion. Excitement. I gravitate toward what calls after me.

Flags offer a sort of invitation, dancing in the wind, a mark of celebration. Red flags are especially enticing with their draw to passion, zeal, and livelihood.

I've heard it said that birds of a feather flock together, and yes, it is true. What I embody is a rare zealous energy. I like to refer to myself as a light, attracting others to safety and warmth, but most assuredly, I also attract bugs. I am a lighthouse as I am created to be, beckoning the lost home to safety, to warmth, and to family. It guides and offers hope to the weary lost at sea.

Without an overflowing cup, I've given my whole glass up to those who thirst, and somewhere along the way, I invite them into my thirst. The most beautiful array of crimson could not entice me to stay. It is a temporary excitement. What was built to break us we will stand upon its defeat for "All things work together for good to those who love God, to those who are the called according to His purpose." (Romans 8:28)

My greatest asset not plugged into the right outlet is sure to electrocute. This bliss is temporary, a temptation to take me on a slight detour—always a short-lived distraction to afford one more moment away from the destin(y)ation. It is good that He is faithful to complete good works. "...being confident of this very thing, that He who begun a good work in you will complete it until the day of Jesus Christ." (Philippians 1:6)

Without this assurance, I would have been a light gone dark, dried of oil, perhaps laid to rest in the tragic arms of a crimson tapestry. But God. There exists this void only He can fill—an appetite I cannot fill, yet convincing myself it's not for me. He leaves the ninety-nine for the one. I think of my mind as a garden, and boy, mine is wild—I like it like that. I've never sought to tame the laughter or the free rock 'n' roll spirit thrashing inside of me, but a few weeds have grown out of hand. At times, they've destroyed the fruits of my labor—what was pure and celebratory. These nasty weeds I've yet to be fully rid of, but I know a guy. I have not guarded my heart. I've filled my tank full and drove until I'm on empty—stranded as the one lost sheep. "And if he should find it, assuredly, I say to you, he rejoices more over that sheep than over the ninety-nine that did not go astray." (Matthew 18:13)

What are some of the distractions that have kept you entangled— away from what God is calling you to?

_____

_____

_____

_____

_____

_____

_____

_____

_____

———

Just One More

YOU'RE LIKE A DISTANT MEMORY, one that I forced myself to relinquish. Moments pass with the weight of boulders on my chest as I pass your room. Your room, untouched, unwrinkled, with musky, warm air, closed up for so long. I take a step inside, and I fight the heavy rushing waters bubbling from within my chest up to my throat. I swallow—pretend I can't recall. "Just one more," you say, as I playfully kiss your head. I walk away and close the door only to find that it was the last one—no more.

Here I am, lying awake as tears plunge into my sheets like the drips of a faucet that refuse to cease, no matter the effort to repair. Those distant memories flood my mind like they just passed. Yesterdays I tried so hard to forget. Crawling into bed with us before the break of morning, brushing your fingers against my face as you tenderly tell of your love for me, looking over your shoulder to see if Mommy was watching.

Joy can also be pain, leaving wounds where memories still

remain, rewinding like a tape and replaying every moment as if they were fresh, new. I close my eyes and try to forget you. But, I can't. I never could.

God's love for us is WILD. He doesn't play by the rules. His love takes barren places and makes them beautiful. Memories such as these used to leave a sting on my heart, and while they are bittersweet, I am firm in knowing who I am and who my children are. We all have the same Papa. He can do anything He likes, and for this, I can rest easy. A moment in time, a painful memory doesn't have to live rent-free in our minds. We can choose to look on it with fresh eyes. We can relish in its beauty from a distance rather than being caught up in the pain. It's like observing the thrashing waters of Pacific waves. You can brave it and go in, or you can observe all its splendor from the sand, avoiding the bitter cold.

The Princess Wept

I MOURN THE GIRL WHO was using her lighthouse to attract what her heart desired. She lured men like a siren, only to sing them sweet nothings and send them back to sea. It's obvious I mishandled them, but more so me. I became like a doll to be tossed to and fro, only loved for a moment then off to the shelf I go. Painted-on smile and beauty won't last. I couldn't see that my pain was connected to my past. The blood of Able cried where Cain spilled his life, and just like abandonment, my orphan heart cried. I cried for a man who might see who I am, but I looked for a temporary fix.

I mourn this woman and her "notice me" cries because all she really wanted was a man who saw her light. She is delicate and kind; her heart has oceans of love, but believing in herself is the key to knowing she is enough. Worthy of honor and worthy of praise, she was always meant to shine like a gold band touched by the blaze. It took the refinement to filter her true nature, for this kind of beauty is not surface and has a depth of flavor. Through the process, she found a man who told her not to drop her crown, but her eyes were still blinded by the past. In the breaking, she found a love that would last. Now she waits in her lighthouse for the return of a man who sees deeper than anyone can.

Don't You Forget

How QUICKLY HAVE I FORGOTTEN Your goodness? I've chased down memories of defeat, pain, and anguish only to hide those that remind me of my victories, of who You say You are. What is this sabotage inside of me? The war is finished but you must believe you are free. Tales of captivity are told where prisoners are no longer shackled yet they remain kept behind bars. What you believe, you will become. "For as he thinks in his heart, so is he." (Proverbs 23:7)

It is self-fulfilling prophecy. What is this flesh that it boasts against the spirit—leading us to and away from, whispering who we are?

"I say then: Walk in the Spirit, and you shall not fulfill the lust of the flesh. For the flesh lusts against the Spirit, and the Spirit against the flesh; and these are contrary to one another, so that you do not do the things that you wish." (Galatians 5:16–17)

Surely I do not believe I know better than the Creator. Surely such pride would crumble before me leading me into a pit of my own making, but mercy and meekness inherit the kingdom of God. You are not God. I am not God.

In Matthew 5, a breakdown is given of inheriting the kingdom of God. Much of these statements reflect a person who has been dumped of self to be filled by God. One who mourns experiences great loss. One who is meek is humble and gentle. They do not seek their own way but lean on His. The peacemakers desire all to have peace, not seeking vengeance but seeing with His eyes. We see folks come in droves to God who have been made empty. Have you ever met someone who went to jail for a while and found God or who experienced a great loss and looked to God? When you have been made empty, you can only be filled. It's a painful place but a fulfilling space.

We have a beautiful identity, and being anyone but our God-given identity robs us of the blessing we have and are to everyone around us. Curiosity killed the cat or maybe the mouse. Mazes of trials occur regularly for scientists. They watch the behaviors of the mice as they are encouraged and discouraged, fed and starved. When finding something good in a maze, we tend to allow a momentary thought to consume us and a perfectly timed distraction to take our eyes off what feeds us. We become bored or afflicted with inner desire and want more.

Have you forgotten His goodness? Have you forgotten His detail and workmanship? What you chase you'll catch up to and you'll get comfortable in that couch—so comfortable that you'll begin to look like it as with the elders on their thrones. Ever wonder where the term couch potato came from? Do not forget His loving kindness. Do not grow weary in doing good.

"And let us not grow weary while doing good, for in due season we shall reap if we do not lose heart." (Galatians 6:9)

Look to where your help comes from. Narcissism is a not-so-scary word, unlike we've made it. It's simply someone who has made their pain an idol. Identifying with what was done to you or what you did is a narrow mindset. Focusing on pain, we move toward it, forgetting His goodness, leaving behind our joys and moments we told ourselves we most surely would not forget. Focusing on pain and a victim mentality, we are rendered useless in the kingdom of God as we can only mirror pain rather than conquer it victoriously. Choose this day whom you will serve. Who said it? Was it God's voice? If not, toss it to the side and move along. Don't look back.

Truly, many scoff at the idea that they'd ever serve another God, but we have all put things above God. I once heard it said that whatever we spend our time, money, and energy on is our God. Yikes! That convicts all of us throughout our lifetime. When we serve our own pain, that pain becomes our God and our identity. Suddenly, we do as it says. We succumb to its every push and pull as we encounter the world around us. The lens we look through becomes one of self-serving pain, and everything is offensive. Truth is offensive. I love the passage that speaks on what we should fill our minds with. Consider Philippians 4:8–9. Give it a read.

A friend of mine taught me something wise. I belt out bellowing cries as I watched the scene of a child being carried away by her abuser in *The Shack*. I turned to my friend recounting things about my own son and his suffering at the hands of evil and my aching to have done something more, to have called the news, pushed harder, anything. What he said was profound and later in another scene repeated by the Holy Spirit and expanded on. He said was something to the effect of "Why do you keep revisiting that?" In a later scene, God spoke clearly to me about how I could not keep looking at the pain or I would drown in it. If you've not watched the movie, I couldn't recommend it enough. In another scene, the main character is in a boat in the middle of the water and begins to be swallowed up by the blackened water, but even as this is happening, forcing its agenda, Jesus is beckoning him. The man listens, and all is made calm.

Truth is like a sword—it cuts down lies. It can be offensive to our flesh, our pre-made-up minds, but pushing beyond it, the humility and desire to grow is a beautiful thing. It's allowing ourselves the chance to rise like a strong sunflower as our Gardener plucks the decay from our leaves.

Don't you forget that your Heavenly Father adores you. A good father wants the best in you. He wants you to grow and flourish. He won't leave you in a dirty diaper to repeat the behaviors that draw ache and pain. He will lay a better path and help you up each time you fall. He will pluck the dead things from your life that will cause distraction and pain.

This friend of mine helped me more than he will know by speaking just as God does to me. Thankfully, I knew the similarity in voice, but I still wrestled with submission for a little while. The song plays on repeat in my mind is "Lead Me" by Sanctus Real. The truth is that when you've known pain for a long time, pain becomes a cruel master you enjoy spending time with. It's familiar. But this pain paints an ugly lens which seeks to rob a brighter future, darkening your gaze. Let Him lead you.

Don't you forget. Play in your mind the memories of His goodness. Jot them down. Look back at notes and photos. Only look to remind of goodness. Don't stay there long. Let us recall the breath of God.

Numb or Somewhere Between?

I HAVE WRESTLED WITH WHETHER God is good for much of my life, noting the unjust things that have happened to myself, my children, and others around me. I've heard pastors talk about our inheritance and the blood shed as if it exempts us from suffering and as if what our lives look like is really just a product of our tongues. I don't believe that, and when those committed churchgoers stop attending much of the time, it has nothing to do with offense and everything to do with erasing their pain with words that don't reflect the Father. They're in a place of wrestling, trying to put off what the world says and instead put on the mind of Christ, but religion, boy, religion.

The ugly in-between of religion seeks to manipulate the Word of God to fit an agenda, and it's been successful for years. It says things like "She did this, so she's..." Our court systems seem to be comprised of religion, lacking all grace and making the person on defense guilty until proven innocent. Rather than coming into a courtroom with an objective mind, lawyers and workers have just returned from breaking bread together and engaging in groupthink. Our family court system does not recognize truth but opinion. If they believe it, with or without proof, it must be true. There is no proving yourself, and when you are innocent, proving yourself is a defeating journey because their minds are already made up. You are guilty, and you did it in the ballroom with the candlestick. I have a nasty habit of making jokes or light of situations that bring about anxiety. Oh, how I despise feeling pinned up against a wall. Try being the one on the stand while everyone in the room has a magnifying glass looking for all your dirt, no matter how unrelated or small. Suddenly, everything they look for is magnified and on blast.

"Everything you say can and will be used against you in the court of law." That sentence has always carried weight for me when thinking about accusation and the way the accuser works on the body of Christ. One wrong move, and I'll throw it back in your face is really what that means. When you are being held under a microscope or magnifying glass, any movement is noted. You walk on a tightrope, hoping you don't fall, and by fall, I mean hold your breath so you don't cry too loudly, speak with too much authority or not enough, or make a single facial muscle movement that could be manipulated. Can you imagine the torment of a courtroom? Accusation. What an ugly matter.

I resonate intimately with the chorus in the song "Somewhere Between" by Henrick. The lyrics talk about that emotionless void where we neither happiness nor sadness. I often feel stuck as I try to contemplate the heart of the Father for me. What is His countenance? I've learned that He is both the Lion and the Lamb. But then I recall all the things permitted in my life. It didn't seem to move anyone one smidge to watch an innocent mother be ripped away from her children. Nothing was done. Not one person spoke up. Not one was held accountable.

I want to believe that God did not forget about what was done to us, every tear and suffering, every question my children may have about "were they loved" and "why did they give me up?" I know I can only run so far on speculation, but NO CHILD deserves to feel that about parents who fought until the bitter end and who lost all their fight against a corrupt system.

Are you still good, God? Did you abandon us? Do you care? I want to believe He has not forgotten, so then if He hasn't, will anything be done? I've been in a holding pattern for over seven years hoping, praying, and standing on the promises of God and remaining strength to sing anyway, to declare anyway, to stand despite.

Many have found more solace in the arms of the bartender or in the lows of a crack house than a church building. Why? Does the church not have a softened heart? Or do we just react with the Word? Do we not contend with and co-pain with the body? If the toe is stubbed, is it not the brain that signals pain?

Many would rather try and function as a single ligament than sit in a pew on Sundays with a face that says all is well when it's clearly not. Yes, sing anyway. Yes, contend for truth anyway despite what we see, but how can a person know the heart of God if not through people? If people do not reflect the heart of God, have we not failed those who yearn for a safe space, for a place to pour their oil, their tears? Stuck between mourning and dancing is not simply focusing on all the pain and praising during the in-between. It's burning for more while waiting. It's desiring the fruit after years of working the fields. This garden has been watered with thousands upon thousands of tears, yet no fruit is harvested. I guess that is a statement with no truth because the fruits of the spirit are long-suffering—check, love—check, joy and goodness—check check. But what I mean by fruit matching up is how long must suffering contend with truth? If You are for me, if You are good, and if what You put together no man can separate all falls flat in my life, then what? I wait, and I've suffered well for nearly seven years. Suffering has a purpose, right? I believe You are good, so surely You have not forgotten us. Surely, you are going to make things right. Surely, this too shall pass. In the in-between, I may mourn one day and dance the next, but I will still yearn for the inheritance you said was mine. The inheritance you gave to me and my loins.

Some time has passed since I wrote the above, and I've realized that my end goal was not God. My hope was not in the Promise Keeper. The end goal was a husband to replace the marriage I lost and a homecoming for the children stolen. My hope was in the promise itself, not the Promise Keeper. *Believe*, a song by Blessing Offor, bears witness to this very thing when the lyrics ask what we want—God or what He can do? That song resonates with the pits of my pain, years of waiting, and not realizing that the moments of God could have been a lifestyle.

This life affords many gods, and those gods are things and people that take precedence over God in our lives. If statements like "If you don't do this, God, you aren't good" sound familiar, chances are you have been playing God with the notion that unless it's your way it won't work out. How about this statement: "I don't know what I'd do without you; I can't lose you"? That statement can be found in the fabric of many relationships these days. It sounds heartfelt, but it reveals who is on the throne of their life. If that person left, and the other one fell apart, their hope and trust was in that person. We can easily be ensnared by putting our hope and trust in what is fleeting, and when that person leaves or the situation doesn't work out, we fall apart. We must be cautious to build our foundation on the solid rock, not one that will make us more broken than when we started.

If we built our homes with straw, like one of the little pigs in the nursery rhyme, not only would the wolf come and blow the house down, but everything inside would be damaged by the wind. God is our insurance for when we don't build the correct way, and He is also the foundation. If we got it right and made Him the foundation, leaning on His understanding, asking Him, letting Him be the love of our lives, then the house wouldn't be knocked down by the winds, and we wouldn't have to tap into that insurance.

It's ironic, really. My heart's desire was always that my children would see the love of God in and through. That prayer and that desire have begun to unfold, to be tangible. My son, Emerson, mimics me. He sings little songs and has a hunger for Jesus at only four years old. I believed the lie from time to time that it had nothing to do with me, but a child often mimics the example given. He sings and paints just like I do. He is excited by his toddler Bible and sharing what he has learned. It does my heart so good to bear witness to this. We won't ever be perfect parents. We won't always say the right thing or do the right thing. But we have both a strong foundation and insurance that is sure and faithful.

After losing everything and replaying the lies I was so

accustomed to hearing for years in a courtroom, I started to believe them. At times I emotionally shut out my son, the very miracle God used to save my life. He would spill something, and the chaos of my heart would become irritated—How could you spill that? Were you watching what you were doing? I still heard the conviction of the Lord and quickly apologized and hugged my son, but I couldn't give the initial grace that I felt had been drained from me. We cannot give our children what we don't have. Each parent has these contradictions they walk out. They don't believe the Lord loves them without restraint, yet they say they love their kids like that. One day they find that faith tested. The truth of what we believe is tested, and we find out quickly whether we believe it.

I remember watching a Hallmark-type movie during high school. A teenage boy grew up in the church and came out to his parents only to discover the most excruciating religious backlash. Rather than loving him where he was at, the parents put sticky notes all around the house noting Scriptures. They used the Scriptures to condemn their son and his behaviors. The boy ended up moving in with an aunt in the city and finding people who would accept him, but he couldn't stop playing on repeat the lies that something was wrong with him. The example from his parents was that love was conditional, and because of this or that, he was no longer welcome. The boy ended his life by jumping off a bridge. Those parents had their faith tested. Did they believe in God's love, unearned and freely given, or behavior modification?

It's humbling to think that without the Lord we cannot do a thing. We need to allow Him to change us from the inside out. If we don't deal with those lies we are consuming and replace them with truth, they affect our hearts and come back out of us. We end up becoming the very thing we feared most because our focus was on the behavior modification that became our identity.

When learning to drive, we are cautioned not to look at the semis because we will drift toward the thing we focus on. It's the same way with sin. Sin is not just a behavior. That behavior is like the leaves of a weed. To pull a weed, we have to find the roots and pull them.

The Lord brings to remembrance the painful places, if we allow Him, and He shows us the truth. The truth sets us free from the lie we believe. I believed the lie for so long that I wasn't good enough, replaced, a terrible mother. I started to manifest what I believed. I was short-tempered and could only see through a lens of pain.

As cliché as it is, "you cannot love another until you love you" is true. You cannot give something you don't possess. You can repeat what was shown, but until you know something, you can't become it. The more you learn something, the more capable you become to teach it. Don't get stuck in the in-between. Let Him be the living water in those barren places. You may not want to revisit that place, but God desires you to conquer your giants. Fear cannot reign and coexist with faith. It must conquer it. Learn to dance on the plans of the enemy.

Trauma to Triumph

TRAUMA ROBS MEMORIES. FOR ME to recall a joyous event can be a strenuous activity because the way my brain has managed normalcy is by pressing down anything painful, even the bittersweet stuff. So as I recall reuniting with the both of my daughters, Neya and Harper (now Neveya and Elaine), I need to be purposeful in doing so. Reuniting was a highlight of God's love in the last three years, but my mind can fog the things that hurt to protect me daily.

When I saw you both, my daughters, something broke inside me. My eyes welled up with tears, and a boulder was lifted from my heart. Your ringlet curls and tousled braids, curiosity and beauty—I knew in that moment that you were loved, not just by myself and your birth family but by your newly acquired family as well, one who clearly brought you up with care and attention. As I think about the whole picture, I think about the attention that your foster mother must have given to choosing matching dresses to add to your child-like beauty and to braiding your hair, delicately combing it to each side and twirling your curls around her fingers.

As the weight was lifted off my chest, I felt the love of God sweep over me in the moment. Something robbed from me was given back, two someones who I thought I'd never know again, at least not until their early twenties when lies were no longer the only memories at their grasp. Instead, I was met with His goodness for the truth of their adoption and embraced by a woman whom I felt genuine love and understanding for in an immediate miraculous way. Even when I can't see God working, He is because He never stops—the message in worship songs I sang for years came alive in a tangible way that day.

Here I am writing as I used to, before letting my thoughts go silent, my testimony. I have felt a call to write my story, and now I have the passion to write as God shows up, moves mountains, and gives Himself the glory in all things made new. It's funny how He changes the desires of your heart to align with His. My first thought at writing this book was to expose the wrong and to hope to change lives in the process so that others did not endure the same heartache. While the latter remains, the former has changed. I want God to get the glory and to show Himself bigger than my enemies. I want my story of Job, if you will, to be pressed down, shaken together, and running over to abundantly bless "Your family and your children and their children and their children." As strange as it may sound, I knew early on that I would write a book about my testimony, but I didn't know how it would play out. I was so laser-focused on what happened to me that it clouded my vision. God was always there with me, through my childhood, as I accepted Him in a little hut situated in the woods at Camp Wanake. He was there in the trips to youth group in middle school and even younger with my Grandma Vicki and Grandpa Rocky. He was there in every single moment. Having new eyes will set you free from the bondage of thinking you understand all the why's. He gives you a clearer, more refined understanding of what He is doing.

My story contains too many testimonials of God's love and hand on my life to note them all within the binds of this book, but I will continue to share His love wherever I go. This recalling of a memory and His hand in it started the veil being lifted in my life. I was still sorting out His goodness and making Him Lord over my life.

"Therefore, my beloved, as you have always obeyed, not as in my presence only, but now much more in my absence, work out your own salvation with fear and trembling." (Philippians 2:12)

The Blessing

THERE WE WERE SITTING AT a rectangular, faux wood table with our chairs a few inches apart, your foster mother to the right and me across the way. Both my girls were sandwiched in-between on either side. I asked you Neveya what her favorite worship song was. At first, you said, "Jesus Loves Me."

I chuckled and said, "You know, that used to be your brother Elijah's favorite song. Yours was 'This Little Light of Mine.' What is your favorite church worship song?"

Your mother, let's refer to her as your mother too, chimed in by asking you as well, trying to dig at what she already knew was your favorite. You didn't reply, looking puzzled. She asked, "The Blessing?"

There you were in agreement.

In amazement, I said that that song brought a life-changing moment. "I heard that song live at Elevation Church, and it was everything to me. It brought me to tears many times."

Your mother said that you all watched it live that day too.

This song was one I sang with assurance and hope, rocking back and forth, singing with tears streaming down my face. To know that my daughter had such love for it too and that you all were watching at the same time brought God's plan full circle!

Wasted Rain

I feel afraid that this blessing God gave me will wither away from my thoughts like the way trauma had been pressed down, locked up, and forgotten in my mind. I don't know what to do with it, because it is a spark of joy that is out of reach, 2,500 miles exactly. Your smiles and laughter should fuel a desire for change, an appetite for movement, but I am back to being paralyzed by fear. God moved on hearts for years at a time, and I am undeserving. I am not obedient, and much of the time His words fall on deaf ears. Sometimes I feel like Te Fiti with my rage and pain too big to defeat. (In the Disney film *Moana*, Te Fiti was made into a different, volcanic identity instead of the green goddess flowing with milk and honey that she was. Her identity changed once her heart was stolen.) My anger is volcanic, and it burns those around me as I feel trapped without words to speak.

I remember seeing *Moana* when it came out, and one scene shook everything inside me. Moana walked through the waters toward what she could have feared. She sang about not being defined by what happens. I hardened my heart to protect myself, and really, it was rare that I could feel because, when you shut out one thing, you shut out all. The message of the song is you are not what was done to you, where you come from, or what anyone says of you. You are not your behavior. You are who God says you are. Don't waste the rain. His promises are sure, and even if it looks like it, if it doesn't line up with what God says, look to where your help comes from. This movie scene is so profound, especially when Moana walks through parted waters. It reminds me of Moses and the parted waters. He obeyed the Lord, and the sea obeyed God inside of him.

"When you pass through the waters, I will be with you; and through the rivers, they shall not overflow you. When you walk through the fire, you shall not be burned, nor shall the flame scorch you." (Isaiah 43:2)

What prompted this writing was someone in my life saying, "God gave you this blessing. What are you doing with it?"

For the first time since my children were taken, I saw my daughters. It felt like torment. I lived in Washington state while they remained in Ohio. Fear had a vice grip on my life. If it weren't for God giving me Emerson, I would have ended my life jumping off that hospital building. My vision was blinded by pain so much that I felt my identity was robbed from me.

Yes, a heinous crime was committed against my family, but its influence over me didn't have to be as great as I made it. My children and husband should not have been my identity. To some effect, they were not as God carried me through the most difficult flames I could have imagined for my life. Now, looking at me, you can't see what I've experienced. Most don't believe I've birthed five children nor that I've endured the pain I have—because I don't look like it. Instead of the mask I wore as a child through learning religion and behavior modification, my joy is true. It is honest and given through great pains in life.

What I am doing now with these blessings, all of the collections of His goodness? I am sharing them with the world. I will tell of His goodness. I will embody His love.

Hills and Valleys

It's EASY TO SING ABOUT peaks and valleys and praises in the storm, but when you are in the heat of it, it's anything but easy. I've balanced between breaking into who I am in Christ and falling into depression, surrounded by lies, the oppressor, and accuser. I often felt entirely empty, but that is what trauma does. It leaves you empty while still feeling the lingering effects of pain and the triggers that snap you back into feeling, usually irrational, angry, or devastated to relive all the moments on repeat, and so the cycle begins again. A path is created much in the same way. If one travels through the woods once, a path is not made for next time. If he then travels the same way on repeat, the path becomes easier to follow.

Trauma is much like this. We become accustomed to the paths of despair we let our minds travel down. I am writing this with the "aha" moment, realizing that God spoke to me a couple weeks ago to study about taking captive my thoughts and bringing them into alignment, and I did not. I studied for one night and then skipped a few, and before I knew it, I was two weeks out of Bible study with a quick-to-anger, low, depressed old self to show for it. For that reason, I will be intentional about studying how I take captive my thoughts and uncover the truth of Job's story, one God continues to draw me toward.

So many years have passed since losing my kids, and it feels like a distant hell, like I took hell and buried it in my backyard. Yet it looks to be taking over my house now. I thought I could plant a few flowers on top and no one would notice, but here I am. As I look out my back door, there it remains festering and still as real as ever.

This realization happened about three years ago. When I read some of these excerpts, they feel like an encounter with a stranger. I'm tempted to erase it and write anew what I know to be true, but I want to leave everything intact. I know this book will touch people in different stages of their faith journey, so for this I leave it intact as written.

Tucked Away

AT TIMES, I TUCK YOU away for safekeeping. It's as if sharing your memory somehow takes from the life of our memories, somehow silences the laughter or numbs the pain. It is all stowed away like precious jewels. Like a car whose value diminishes as it leaves the lot, I often hide your person, your spirit—even your face—from my mind because I don't want to share you with another or cut who you were in half with the moment experienced. I used to think I was repressing the pain and sorting through trauma. I suppose I was, but more than that, I was caring for those flames and ensuring they aren't extinguished so that they remain intact, precious, and untouched—not tarnished by today. I know I can't keep you tucked away forever. Eventually, you will each grow to new heights and experience new depths, and maybe I'll be kept in your safe space or maybe I'll be taken along to experience. Either way, it is in God's hands, and He knows your hearts far better than I can hope.

Not too many parents experience the bitter feeling of giving a child over to God until they must. Children are a heritage, an inheritance, unearned and freely given. Knowing exactly what He is doing, why would we need to give them back? For some time, playing back memories in my mind, as good as they were, was torment. Something remained just out of reach though they played like a movie reel—even more so tangible like I could reach out and grab a hug or jump into a birthday scene. A release was needed. I couldn't keep playing these moments like a loop in my mind, eating up all my strength and hope.

Hours would turn into days, and having my son, Emerson, only beckoned more of a catch and release for holding that fish would rob my breath. Emerson's quirks, giggles, and nuances were so familiar, so like each of my children, and my joy would be painted over with sorrow. Suddenly, I'd be taken on a ride down memory lane as Em would flicker his eyelashes a certain way or utter a word that defied his age in wisdom. I learned to keep the memories stored in jars until I could open them up without it being a Pandora's box.

The release didn't happen overnight. It was more like a bite at a time. I had worries that filled in the gaps of not knowing. That was probably the worst. Fear sought to choke out the faith I had. They couldn't coexist. One must defeat the other, and most of the time it felt like fear was the heavyweight champion. A nugget of truth would birth when understanding God's love for me, knowing that He loves them more than I could hope to. Another revelation would pepper my mind with knowing they too hear from God—they are not alone. What held my mind captive wasn't the memories but the blanks I was filling in. Where are they? Who are they? Do they fill in the blanks in their minds, assuming there must be something wrong with them for this to happen? Are they safe? Loved? Bullied? I was desperate for release at times. I learned to speak over my mind and over my children what God says. That is where the thoughts of fear, my Goliath, went running as faith plucked up every weed in my mental garden.

Being defined by something other than what God says can be hindering. Now, rather than hearing what He says, we have our minds made up. This is what happened when I had counselors suggest PTSD, ADHD, and medication. Eventually, I folded, and for a while, the medication was helpful until it wasn't. I am not dogging anyone's use of mediation temporarily. For me, it became a crutch and an excuse to live in bondage to the mind. I wanted to be so reliant on what God said that no longer was I held at gunpoint by a thought. Yes, it felt that oppressive at times. Over the years, I slowly learned to make God's Word the authority in my life. It took some time because I had some nasty weeds (lies) that had overtaken my garden (mind).

I learned to unpack what I had tucked away, unseal those jars, and let the memories breathe. They didn't have to stay there, but I had to know what to do with them. With time, over the span of nearly seven years, I released my children through songs, poems, narrative, painting, and anything I could to preserve my love for them.

Found In

GOD IS IN THE HIDDEN places, the don't-want-to-know or don't-care-to-know, concealed ugly places we discard because they are not pleasant to look at or to listen to, the cries bellowing up and pouring out in the shower, the laughter that catches the wind when we see a flicker of hope and joy in a child while enduring heartache.

He is in the small moments, the stillness, the aches. When we are weak and we fall at His feet, He is our strength in our time of need. He doesn't want a show and pleasantries; leave them at the door. Sure, we have hope, joy, and peace, access to the most nourishing fruits, but suffering is love too. Was it not Jesus who cried out on the cross "Forgive them for they know not what they do"? Was it not His sacrifice that reflected the true heart of love on the darkest day this world has known?

We don't have to conceal the pain, but we also don't have to live in it, break bread with it, or lie with it. We can acknowledge its existence and thank God anyway. We can rest in His heart and His love when we don't have the strength to run. It's there we are given a helper to lift us up.

When life hasn't caught up to the promise God gave you, stand anyway, sing anyway. A glass bottle reflects light, but when we give our broken pieces to God, the light reflects, zigs and zags, pieces through. It's intoxicating to acknowledge the God of the universe through heart-wrenching pain. The light breaks through the darkness. For even on the darkest day, love broke through, mercy rained down, and the stone was rolled away!

Mama Bear

HELL HATH SEEN NO FURY until it has come face to face with a mama bear. You ever wonder why we don't hear of a papa bear? Mamas are connected to their babies no matter where in space and time they may be. A mama's heart-wrenching cry mimics God's love He has for us. Mothers are an example of love as tangible as we have to grasp here on earth. When her babies become a part of the war, the battle awakens inside of her.

Have you ever met the eyes of a woman who has lost a child? Do you know the deep well of pain that swallows her up? I have woke to shrill cries in my heart imagining the pain eating up my babies. I have held them in my heart when they aren't here. I have sat thousands of miles away, knowing that my God won't let us go.

Even If

You'll love me when I'm broken—when I feel not enough.
Even when I feel like I should just give up.
All my hope is fading. Are you sure you didn't leave?
What is this endless love? Are you sure it's for me?
I have known replacement, to be left behind,
always looking backward trying to rewind.
Like where are all my memories, buried deep inside.
I won't let you see the heartache that I'm tryin' to hide.
You love me when I'm broken—when I feel not enough.
All these voices gettin' louder—they just won't give up.
Bullies at the bus stop—no voice to say enough.
These places are inside me though heaven knows
I've tried to paint a picture of the future in my mind.
I tried. I tried.
You love me when I'm broken—when I feel not enough.
You find me in the wreckage, and You say it is done.

For Just a Moment

For Elijah & Tristen
What I wouldn't give to buy time.
I'd give all my savings, every ounce of breath I've left
to see you once more.
There's a void in my chest.
It's been too long, my dear,
and my tears have grown many.
I'll wake up one day
and you'll have aged twenty.
If I could take just one moment to say all there is to say,
I'd have to stop time,
because there are mountains I've prayed.

I've prayed for your safety and blessings on blessings.
I hear your cries in the night.
Somehow I know what your heart says.
I want to fill your void too with a great big hug and a cry,
but this pain will end soon.
It will soon be our time.
So until we meet, I'll leave you to our Maker.
He knows all you need, and He'll always be your caretaker.

Consider What Is Wild

PATIENCE IS MADE EVIDENT IN the waiting. Waiting has never been my strong suit. I find myself gripping the steering wheel, itching for more control in a traffic jam and in life. I keep myself busy to avoid the wave of emotions I am evidently treading—barely.

No matter the boat or rescue sent to me, I'd rather exert all the strength left in me to stay at the surface. In the stillness, I find myself wrecked with the uncertainty. Didn't you say? Didn't I hear that firmly in my spirit? But You are God, and I am not. Your ways are not my ways. My timeline does not look like the standard—first marriage, a house, and then kids. For that I have remained frustrated at what I see as wreckage. Not enough. Damaged.

The truth is, pain has long been my friend, the only confidant at times. It's consistent and trustworthy. It won't leave me or abandon me. It knows things of me that others refuse to see. Breathing paves the way for clarity as the brain recovers more oxygen and the frontal lobe is no longer at war with the consciousness, chaotically focusing on emotional reaction.

Rachel Morley's song "Ever Present, Always True" has thrashed through my impenetrable walls for as long as I've discovered it. The lyrics penetrate depths I forgot exist inside of me. Intentionality is a choice to spend time valuably. I am a wildflower—a little estranged, a little misunderstood but beautiful still. I exist to soak up the Son and take up space in the most unlikely spaces. Wild and free. My true form. Consider the wildflowers, I will.

The Power of Memory

OUR MEMORY CALLS TO REMEMBRANCE the goodness of the Lord. Written on our hearts are words of life and breakthrough, images of laughter and dance, song and praise. A mind submitted to the Lord is clay, molded and redefined. Remember, don't you forget— Lay aside the cobwebs and darkness seeking to cloak the light. I will remember You from the moment of my first heartbeat to the kicking feet from inside my womb. The tiny fingers and eyelashes. The longing little girl inside of me who is beckoned to her papa, never forgotten. Each tear collected to be as rains of blessing and praise. We uphold His name on the sounds of our praise as we recall. Always remember.

The Earth remembers the creatures big and small as they are laid to rest, a foundation to feed generations to come. Our ancestors paved paths of old. History is alive in our blood. It's alive in the waters and in the soil. All of the earth groans for the Lord, singing and praising. The stars reverberate; the trees shake; the waters roar. What the Lord is speaking in and through creation has no cap. Let not your mind forget. Let your lips continue His praise. Be given unto new eyes and near ears. For the day at hand calls for necessity what the things of old laid the path for.

Our minds are beautiful places, and the Lord gave us memories to recount the goodness of His character. When yielded to pain rather than submission to our papa, it takes us to depths we didn't want to journey. We are like fish traveling in packs, not overcome by the waters, and the sun breaking through. Along comes an untimely meal, and we excite at what doesn't immediately look like bait. We swim speedily for it, realizing only after what intention lie beneath. We are hooked and being pulled to and fro with no control. This analogy of bait could be used to speak to several kingdom principles, but consider the mind. If we are allowing ourselves to be sucked into the mental despair of a previous experience, we are now signed up for a baited adventure that is anything but fun. Submitting our minds is vital as our mind tells us which way to go and what to speak. Whatever the mind is submitted to, you'll see manifest in your life, similar to the heart as our words tell of what lay hold its possession.

"A good man out of the good treasure of his heart brings forth good; and an evil man out of the evil treasure of his heart brings forth evil. For out of the abundance of the heart his mouth speaks." (Luke 6:45)

"…casting down arguments and every high thing that exalts itself against the knowledge of God, bringing every thought into captivity to the obedience of Christ." (2 Corinthians 10:5)

First Love

MY FIRST LOVE TOOK MY heart at a pre-pubescent age, a little fearful, awestruck, and enamored by a kind of love that unashamedly looked on me with pride and adoration. Found in a little hut situated in the middle of the woods, sounds of gentle weeping and crickets, You saw me.

The invitation and impression were one of soft peace and palpable joy. I could reach out and touch You, take care to an omitted hug, and listen intently for the edification desperately desired. Leaving behind my father and mother, I became your bride, You my home. Every void running over with agape love and grace sufficient for all things.

Never to forget my first love, I took care to place you on a shelf and dust you off from time to time. You became an afterthought as adolescent pressure and passions swept me into confusion. A revival to awake me and a spirit-filled service brought me back for a moment of reconciling. And again, you were like a forgotten toy I didn't have time or interest in playing with anymore.

When tragedy struck and lay hold, every heartache and pain became a daily hell. I buckled under the weight of it. I cried out and blamed You for abandoning me, for permitting such heinous crimes. Justice was not my portion. This long-lost friend was someone I had forgotten. I couldn't recall the washing of peace like sitting by the riverside or the joy that bubbled up from my chest. I was defeated by corruption and a raping of innocence.

In the wreckage, You reached out Your hand, and I accepted the call back home. I didn't come home running to You or missing Your touch at first. I shamefully came, aching for truth as words of slander and accusation took hold of my home. Did I become the massage parlor my husband snuck off to? Like a geisha, I entertained men with songs and sensuality, men who did not mirror the Groom. But, my first love met me with open arms like the prodigal son, offering pride and joy, adoring every moment returned to His arms.

I love you, Mommy

"I LOVE YOU, MOMMY." THOSE were the words I thought that I'd always play on repeat, sweet as honey pouring from your lips—honey that would always sweeten my day. But that honey ran dry, and I don't recall the last time I heard those words.

You didn't leave this world. You didn't run from me or hide. You were stolen from my arms to silence the bellowing cry of love that once poured from the walls of our house. Dancing in the kitchen. Bedtime stories and tuck, tuck, tuck giggles.

We get used to hearing the same words so much that they become background noise until they are no longer there and their silence leaves us aching for the room in our mind they once took up.

I love you—three simple words that warmed even the coldest winter day. I love you meant so much more before I became the throwaway. You were a gift to my bosom—one I may have grown used to, but I search through memories to hear " I love you" once more. All the ways—it went without saying. All the ways we loved.

"Your babies are my babies." No matter the distance or loss of time, moments, and I love you's, the authority over my children remains the Lord's. I won't ever stop believing, praying, or standing in the gap for my bloodline. Change their names, take them from my arms, but my blood is theirs. My heart once beat next to theirs connected by cord and spirit always. I will declare breakthrough, peace, and joy running over. I will not relent. I will not be silent in my efforts to proclaim the truth of what God says. He gave me those babies because they needed me and I them. Let nothing separate what God has put together.

By Choice

YOU MAY NEVER KNOW SOME people, not because you didn't go out on a limb or outstretch your arm, but because they didn't want to be known. Being vulnerable has its pains and fears of rejection, but it swings wide open the opportunity for the right people to invite you in and to know the depth of who you are—the depth of who they are. It's an exchange of vulnerability. You cannot be known unless you are willing to be hurt. To be known is to share your heart's cry—giving a glimpse of what lies beneath the surface. If you are comfortable enough or bold enough in your own skin, others will be showered in your authenticity, and in your truest form, your inner child shines through. Don't worry, darling, about those who seek to live in the dark, but remain as a light. Let your light shine, and step into the dark to change the atmosphere. Even the dimmest light will ravage the darkness.

This choice to be known shows the need for inviting the Lord into our life. We have options, and the choice is entirely ours. Do we take a risk and let Him in or do we keep Him out? What do you have to lose but your chains? What do you have to gain but everything else? Why does Jesus need an invitation to come in? Love is a choice.

It's not threatened nor controlled or else it wouldn't be love. God gives us the choice to accept Him or reject Him. When we choose Him, it is like connecting with an old friend. Suddenly, as we open the door to our heart, we reminisce of old memories, and it dawns on us that He was always there. A memory of chance becomes awakened to truth. You begin to see all the opportunities extended to you for love, for joy, and for peace. God never withheld from you, but He is a gentleman, and love is a choice. We are afforded the option of choosing our own way or His way. Choose this day.

Which path do you want to take?

_____
_____
_____
_____
_____
_____
_____

Do memories come to mind when you think back on His goodness?

_____
_____
_____
_____
_____
_____
_____
_____
_____
_____
_____
_____

I Saw That

WE HAVE ALL COME ACROSS the "I saw that" stickers with a look of judgment from the Father. We see them plastered at the subway station, on telephone poles, and overwhelmingly available on social media for purchase. When I think of the Lord, I think of a different vantage point—one where He sees the beginning from the end, the detours, and the destination. He is like a bird soaring above all things good and evil, blessed and shamed. Only He has eyes on everything.

For many years, I've been enamored with birds. They can travel in groups, taking care of their young, and building with what they are freely given. They do not have to work for a thing.

"Look at the birds of the air, for they neither sow nor reap nor gather into barns; yet your heavenly Father feeds them. Are you not of more value than they?" (Matthew 6:26)

This Father is a good one. He reveals to redeem. If there is correction, it is for protection, always. He desires your heart, and if it is hardened, harming self or others, it's got to be made new.

"I will give you a new heart and put a new spirit within you; I will take the heart of stone out of your flesh and give you a heart of flesh." (Ezekiel 36:26)

Recalling Pharaoh, a heart of stone will gain you nothing. It keeps out everything, like the word *offense*. It sounds a lot like "a fence." Offense is "a trap" and also defined as a stumbling block, a snare. The origin word *chattaah* translates to "sin" and "offense." A hardened heart or an offended heart misses the blessing. Why?

Think on this, if God uses people as blessings...

"But God has chosen the foolish things of the world to put to shame the wise, and God has chosen the weak things of the world to put to shame the things which are mighty." (1 Corinthians 1:27)

God uses people. Recall God hardening Pharaoh's heart. He hardened the heart of Pharaoh who came after the Israelites so that His will could be fulfilled, so that all glory would go to Him as the Israelites met an impossible fate, but yet they did not and Moses said to the people, "Do not be afraid. Stand still, and see the salvation of the Lord, which He will accomplish for you today. For the Egyptians whom you see today, you shall see again no more forever." (Exodus 14:13)

Moses asked the people to stand still. This reminds me of "Be still, and know that I am God. I will be exalted among the nations, I will be exalted in the earth!" (Psalm 46:10)

He is our refuge and strength. All things work together for the good of those who love the Lord and are called according to His purpose, right? Yes, so then everything in this earth serves Him. Since you are a joint heir to His throne, everything then also belongs to you. The trap set before the Israelites by the Egyptians became their very own trap as the waters overcame them. They thought that backing the Israelites into a corner, so to speak, was wise, but they didn't know the God the Israelites served. Let's revisit and continue on to what happened that day at the parting of the Red Sea. Exodus 14:14 continues on with "The Lord will fight for you, and you shall hold your peace." A few verses later we find "Then Moses stretched out his hand over the sea; and the Lord caused the sea to go back by a strong east wind all that night, and made the sea into dry land, and the waters were divided." (Exodus 14:21)

Notice what had happened was linked to obedience and stillness.

What has God asked you to do? What did He say about it?

_____
_____
_____
_____
_____

No matter what it looks like, be still and know that He is Lord! The purpose of obedience is to show goodness to His children. His vantage point is different from our own. Where we see enemies, He sees opportunities. In Exodus, we see how the very trap laid before the Israelites was what trapped their enemies. But, it does not end there. There was a point to prove. The Word says, "He permitted no one to do them wrong; Yes, He rebuked kings for their sakes, Saying, 'Do not touch not My anointed ones, and do My prophets no harm.'" (Psalm 105:14-15)

To each judgment, there is a purpose as there is with favor. "And we know that all things work together for good to those who love God, to those who are the called according to His purpose. For whom He foreknew, He also predestined to be conformed to the image of His Son, that He might be the firstborn among many brethren." (Romans 8:28–29)

Consider then the cross. The cross is vertical and horizontal in its design. The vertical represents our connection with the Father above us, and the horizontal is the connection with people, the relatability of a testimony for the purpose of delivering the heritage. Jesus died for all not just the well-behaved, the every Sunday churchgoer, or the labeled "Christian." He died so that we might have perfect union with Him so that as we abide in Him, He abides in us. The more we spend time with Him, the more we look like Him.

Behavior modification in your own strength will render you entirely undone for "My grace is sufficient for you, for My strength is made perfect in weakness." (2 Corinthians 12:9) If you are so strong and can do it all yourself, what need do you have of the Lord? When we submit ourselves to the Lord, seek His face, repent, and turn from our ways, the veil of lies is lifted and we start to see Him at work everywhere. We must be emptied of ourselves to be filled with all He is because His desire is that we look like Him to influence another to look like Him. We cry out in the impossible so that He can answer our cry and make it possible. We are dumped of our own power and authority and replace them with His power and authority. What comes after pride? The fall. He wants us to submit to Him like we submit to any good father or husband as He is good and only has good things for us. We won't believe that unless we have spent time with Him and we know His character. Who would do a trust fall with a stranger.? I don't think I would.

This fire-and-brimstone God we have all come to fear is not so fiery. He is both the Lion and the Lamb. The Lion is the authority and the Lamb is love and grace. So pair the two and you have the perfect household, the perfect parents. Judgment does exist, yes, but for correction. He does not desire any of His kids to be apart from Him. He sent His Son as a sacrifice to tear the veil so that ALL have access to this WILD love. It is written, "If My people who are called by My name will humble themselves, and pray and seek My face, and turn from their wicked ways, then I will hear from heaven, and will forgive their sin and heal their land." (2 Chronicles 7:14)

What did we just uncover about sin? Sin and offense are closely related, aren't they? What areas of your life have you not handed over to God—the ones you think you know best in? Those areas are where your heart is hardened, preserving your own traditions, understanding, and selfish pain rather than letting God tear down those walls and heal what's inside. Allowing Him to work stops the pattern from repeating. You get the healing, and suddenly you carry that testimony (to do with the same power and authority) into every room you enter.

If you desire to heal others, to love on them, and to be His hands and feet, you cannot do it until your walls are down and you allow Him to heal your heart. For if your walls remain up, your heart is closed off to people and to God. In that space is where "For the thing I greatly feared has come upon me, And what I dreaded has happened to me" becomes alive. (Job 3:25)

If your fear is bigger than your faith, it must be tested. Nothing but the Lord is to have dominion and authority in your life—no fear, no man, no word but all that God is and all that He says. If you are shattered and not made whole, everywhere you move you'll cut everyone on that broken glass. Don't believe me? Let me show you.

If a woman who is carrying around her pain from childhood desires to work with children and does not heal those places in her heart, she will cut every child in her path on her broken pieces. The Word says out of our hearts flow the issues of life. So a man thinks he is. Faith comes through hearing. If you still have brokenness in your heart, everything flows from it. Suddenly, everything and every child that woman sees helps remind her of what she experienced.

She isn't looking at truth; she is looking through broken glass. Girl, allow God to make you whole! Even that contradiction is meant to be under your feet. He placed it on your heart to work with children, but the testing produces the testimony. Allow Him to do the work so that you can effectively do the work. It's not so hard when you've healed because now all that you do flows from healing, not pain.

So then, "I saw that." Yeah, He did, and His goal is not behavioral modification but healing and restoration to bring back together everything that has been broken. Why else do you think He defeated the grave? He defeated the grave so that "death is swallowed up in victory." Our enemies are not flesh and blood but principalities and powers. Who was the snake in the garden? A liar. A liar can only lie. The Holy Spirit is truth, and every other spirit is a lie. What lie are you holding onto that seeks to choke out the truth? The truth will set you free. Don't look at your brother and see the plank in their eye but look at your own. Can you control another? No, but you can change you. You can dig deep into what is affecting your walk and your vision. What are you thinking on, and who said it? What memory are you revisiting? What is it birthing in your mind?

Someone who has been given the sickness PTSD revisits painful memories, memories that tell a story evoking anger, pain, helplessness, unrest, and shame. Is that your portion? The Word says "… whatever things are true, whatever things are noble, whatever things are just, whatever things are pure, whatever things are lovely, whatever things are of good report, if there is any virtue and if there is anything praiseworthy—meditate on these things." (Philippians 4:8)

What do you look back on in your mental rearview?

_____

_____

_____

What is the lie or pain standing in the way?

_____

_____

What unforgiveness and bitterness are you holding?
What is it attached to? Where did it make its home?

_____

_____

_____

_____

_____

_____

_____

How do you pull a weed if not by its roots? Take that to the Lord. That is what God wants to heal—the very thing you build walls around to protect, but GOD! You cannot keep the bandage on for forever, hoping it will somehow heal a festering wound. The longer you leave that wound hidden beneath the bandage, the worse it gets. This is what the test looks like. All is meant to be under our feet just like our Papa's, but if we are going to make a molehill a mountain, it's going to take some releasing to deal with that thing. I know a guy. He can move the mountains. He can and has moved the sea.

The truth will set you free. Let go of your vice grip on the lie. You were never meant to hold on for forever. Letting go is meant to produce a testimony of victory so that others can walk that same path you cleared for them. Do you want to be well?

Settling

SETTLING IN, NESTLING IN CLOSE, and trying to forget is comforting, but soon the days turn into weeks, then years, and before I know it, I've submitted my whole life to what was. I must allow the Lord to gather the loose strings of my heart.

Settling was familiar and confused with rest. I've allowed it to rob the passion beating inside my chest. I've erased parts of myself and hid others away to try and fit into this tiny box I've made. It changes its shape and its size depending on the me I'm trying to fit inside.

Peace, quiet the thoughts bursting from my mind. I've discovered how to barricade them outside. With walls of steel arming my heart, I could not perceive the new thing, Your restart.

If I passed rest on the street, I wouldn't know his name, because I've avoided a brush with stillness all the same. As a little girl, I dreamed of settling down, assured that this accomplishment would be my crown.

But I don't want to settle. I want rest in my heart. I want to dance with my fears knowing they won't tear me apart. I've settled with chances I refused to take. I've settled in chains I thought I would break. I've found settling to be an internal coercion—handcuffed to distortion.

I've disputed the problem inside for too long. There's nothing left to settle—in fact, there's nothing wrong. I was made to shine. I don't want to hide my light. If I have something to say, I won't have to put up a fight. To settle down sounds like comfort and a place to call home, but I've spent years in this hell and I've done it alone. I want more than status quo, more than what meets the eye. I want to take a leap of faith and soar through the sky!

Tolerated

I REMAIN TOLERATED IN A room with mindless chatter, whispering name-calling the cause, exalting self while I slumber. This kind of sleeping drowns out the proverbial truth lurking in the room, asleep to noises that call out fear, that beckon truth. I've spent a lifetime here, and I've felt like Aurora always awaiting her prince to come and rescue her, but perhaps no one is coming. Tolerant—never agreeing to my person. Her laugh. Her love. Her grace. Her clothes. Never quite fitting in but determined to stand out from this place of swelling destiny. She remains dormant in familiar comfort to exist with those who look right through her. I have itched to become a part of the conversation, rubbing sleep from my eyes, but when I stumble in, I too become dressed in lies. I begin feeding on the stuff of mice—eating slander and hooded affection. I leave feeling sick. What have I done? This chatter. Always chatter. How's it been? How's your neighbor?

This emblematic sleep refers to a monster sweeping nations, all-consuming. In which case, I'm wide awake. When trying in vain to carry this heaping truth upon my back, I stumble and return to soft words and comforting hands, leading me back to the lies I've slept with from my genesis. In a moment I am made alive like Lazarus only sleeping. No tolerating what He made but jubilant love flowing in and through me. I humbly hand the burden to Him, to have and to hold. My strength can't bear it alone. This weight I've carried became my home. So here am I, send me, in an effortless flight as I take to the deep, soaring on your wings. Flying can be accomplished outside of dreams.

Love doesn't tolerate—it celebrates.

Unbelievable

"CAUSE EVEN WITH GOOD PEOPLE, even with people you can kind of trust, if the truth is inconvenient, and if the truth doesn't, like fit, they don't believe you." - "Unbelievable"

With all the false evidence stacked up and a broken spirit left behind, those I thought were supposed to love me, to protect me, to speak for me, or at least show up, didn't. Words are a powerful force, and waking to the sound of no follow-up text or call, no slight curiosity of how you're doing from those who braided your hair, tucked you in, and laughed and cried with you really is the worst abandonment. One could argue in defense of a lack of what to do or say, but in those moments, nothing is the loudest void. Strangers showered me with the love and grace of God, speaking to liven my aching soul and dying spirit. Strangers looked upon me, and saw my authentic form, blameless and without reserve.

I found this sort of love, or rather, it has sought me out time and again, to wash away the disdain of human failure and replace it with an unearned favor and love. My Father adores me. He looks at me with love. It's not our job to determine whether someone is right or wrong, picking them apart and deciding how much of your love they deserve. Our job is to love others, right where they stand, no matter on the mountaintop or deep in the underbelly of pain.

"Will they believe me?" It's a tale as old as time ringing loudly for rape victims. I once had a woman refer to my story as a rape. Yes, this place penetrated my family, robbed our life, and forced our silence under the mask of shame. The injury could be felt like a stone tossed in an evergreen lake, rippling for generations. This was unlawful. This was a violation. The unbelievable still happens. Don't make someone's inconvenient truth something they feel responsible to swallow.

Let us posture our hearts in such a way that we see through His lens, one not riddled with our own pain and perspectives we have dug up through tunnels of regret and trauma in our minds. Let your mind be renewed by His spirit so we can look on one another with the love of God. Are they not His children? Did Jesus also not die for Judas? Wanting the cleansing and healing power of the Lord is easy. Why wouldn't we accept such a gift? The true testing of faith is loving the Judas. We are called to love as He loves. We are called to give grace as He gives us freely. If we have it, we are called to give it, period. While many abandoned me, the Lord did not, and I found Him in the depth of surrendering. I was poured out—all of me. Only then can we be filled back up. We go through things that are not fair, that are pure evil. Do you recall Judas? He sold Jesus out for some coins, and in the end, it didn't matter.

Like Chapstick is a balm for dry places, oil fills what is barren. God desires to wash over those hidden spaces. We've got to give Him all the places, good, bad, and ugly. He doesn't just want what looks pretty. Don't you know, He can tell when you are pretending. You don't have to be strong with Him. In our weakness, He is made strong. Let Him take all those places that no one wants to visit—the barren, the riddled with tumbleweed, lacking water or fruit. He wants those places. You are the church, and you take Him everywhere you go. How relatable are you if all the walls are up, hoarding pain like everything is perfect? I'll let you in on a little secret, we are all always being refined, corrected, molded, and made new. It's a daily thing. At times, the sun looks a little brighter, and other days rains keep pouring. Both are okay, but don't sit in those rains for too long. Joy comes in the morning. He trades our mourning for dancing. The rains are used to wash away the facade and reveal the heartache He needs to see to heal. How do you water a flower kept under a porch? You don't. Flowers grow in the rain.

You Are SAFE

WHAT LIVES INSIDE ME FEEDING with an insatiable hunger to be dissatisfied? What is it that fuels the fire of despair to chase after what is off-limits but rather delightfully available? What is it inside that groans for what leaves me unheard, unseen, and not valued? Why is it so difficult to be still? I've developed trails of faith in my mind like those tracked a hundred times, neuropaths that define the road set before me like the one behind.

I rest looking at the glowing sun breaking light through the crown of the trees, letting the wind take hold of my curls and rustle the leaves beneath my feet, catching an earnest childlike wonder to discover what is beautiful by natural design. I tarry through these woods without recognition of time—to be like the wind in movement and like the trickling waters wading in the deep as my toes clench the river's moss-bitten stones.

I've heard that trauma causes us to self-soothe—probably because it is often difficult to communicate such deep and suppressed emotions via social conditioning or masking to protect our current livelihood. I've escaped to fields of flowers with a light breeze catching the hem of my dress, twirling in the sun's rays, jumping and dancing as a tall strong oak provided shade for my leisure.

I learned in my twenties that I developed what is called a "Safe Space." What an incredible concept to know that rather than self-soothing with a method that could have robbed my life, God gave me the gift of natural escape and a desire to fade into the earth like a raindrop that disappears into the soil.

He is such a good God that He sustains us through it. Healing may not happen overnight, but He is still God and still good.

Light up the Dark

It's EASIER TO BLEND IN than stand out.
Don't you know you're a light—don't let it burn out.
You were made to light up the night.
Follow Me wherever you go.
If I am your compass, you'll always have hope.
You're feeling the weight of incompetence.
Don't you know I make beauty of brokenness?
Your fear holds you captive, but it's all a lie.
The shattered parts of you will reflect the light.
Your heart was made for more.
Being a chameleon will close every door.
I know it's easier to blend in than stand out.
You are a never-ending light—smother the doubt.
The fire you have burns through the night,
nothing can extinguish the light that's inside.
Come out from darkness wherever you're hiding,
the light that's within you;
it may be blinding, but roads worth traveling are often dark.
You need my light to uncover your heart.
This part may be lonely—foreign, unknown,
but you'll always have Jesus—your forever home.

Self Sabotage

I FOUND MYSELF LOST A time or two, walking through pain and trying on other shoes.

I kept running away from you. You found me in hiding—desperate for love I searched for in the dark. I was never that girl. I was lost in the world that I had made for myself, but you weren't scared of who I'd become.

I found myself lost a time or two, walking through pain and trying on other shoes.

I always knew what you wanted me to do, but I made the fear a mountain I couldn't climb. I knew I should let go and give it to You, but I didn't want to burden the one who loved me. You love me. I didn't know what love felt like, always trying to fill the void—fighting intimacy.

I found myself lost a time or two. I didn't want to walk through my pain with you.

I was afraid of what you might see—always hiding—empty, waiting. When given the chance, I laced up my shoes and ran from You.

Yes, Jesus Loves Me

ANOTHER NIGHT OF READING *JESUS Loves Me*, a Veggie Tales board book I picked up ahead of all the Easter traffic at Walmart. I breezed through the snoozing dinosaur book with the little energy I have left in the day, a few one-liners and it gets the job done, but the conviction inside doesn't allow me to leave *Jesus Loves Me* incomplete.

So here we are reading the lyrics again, and my son begins pressing the upper right button to hear a muffled song break through the tiny speaker until he has it and starts singing, "Yes, Jesus loves me."

Suddenly I'm back in my leather-seated GMC Acadia looking back at you asking again for your favorite song, the same song you beg for each time I buckle you in. Before I know it, you're belting out those lyrics from a place deep in your belly, "Yes, Jesus loves me."

Your wild love sprung out of cracked windows rolling down Ohio back roads, and I return to Veggie Tales as Emerson reaches to press the button again. Tears roll down my face and I feel the hot sting of pain bubble up again. Where are you? Who are you? Yes, Jesus loves you.

Remember Me

REMEMBER ME ON THE MOUNTAINTOP as you look into the valley. Remember the tears you cried out in desperation. Remember the wilderness and the grip of its darkness. Remember the highs and lows—the deep cries out. I am in My children near and far. Use My spirit to look on the heart. Let your righteousness not blind your humble beginnings, and bless those who curse you. Stand in the gap for those who persecute you—for those who reject you reject Me. You have favor with the Me and among men. Let the anointing you carry spread like wildfire, exposing the hidden things. Some hide in the darkness for comfort being at home with their broken idols. Like Paul, having a thorn in his side, your breakthroughs will be knit together with humility. It keeps you reliant on Me; you cannot run ahead of a whispering voice. Do not be afraid as I go with you. Look to the Son on the mountaintop as My wind blows and guides you. Be still to recall My words and look for what is beautiful. It takes no wisdom to see what is dark. Humility unlocks a washing in the spirit. Let My living water flow down the hill and into the crevices and things deemed "untouchable." I made all the creatures, big and small. Let praise ever be on your lips.

Celebration can blind us from the pain like the holiday lights and laughter while another fades into the background drowning in memories of the past. Don't move so fast. We look forward to driving toward the promise, but some transitions require us to look back for a moment in humility to be appreciative. Yes, the promise is beautiful in all its color, its excitement, a magnificent rainbow. I know you cannot wait to go there, and really, it is not a destination. You take it with you, a little gold to scatter on your way, but relish in the little things. Take notice of the flowers and the smoothed water stones. Don't let well enough alone.

Take inventory of the pain and shame. Make her a new name. Welcome home, my darling, you were never alone. You cannot leave her as she is. She cannot see what you see with joy being temporary. On this journey, you are sure to find pain has placed itself in your luggage. They have names you can't possibly forget though you've tried to bury them beneath the pretty things. Take the time to release the old so that you may relish the new. Daughter, you cannot take those with you. So, forget the girl you used to be but remember your knees. You've dug in the garden long enough to play in the weeds.

Seek the mountain and all her offerings, but look down at how far you've come. Don't forget to celebrate the little victories.

Warring Myself

I'VE BEEN TRYING LIKE HELL to put up a fight.
Forgiveness ain't easy, at least not tonight.
A war I can't win against my own self,
I'm tired and angry trying to figure it out.
Where are you? Where have you been hiding?
I wish I could find you. Your light lights up the room.
Times like these are hard when the tape won't stop rewinding,
Playing the moments I miss the most.
Like how you picked dandelions and swore they were flowers.
How you questioned everything, and your intoxicating laughter.
Your need to know why, and your strong will for adventure.
Your sideways grin you tried to hide deep within you.
You put up a fight just to hide what you feel.
But, little one, don't you know,

you're pouring out love wherever you go?
So go ahead and ask every over-thought question.
Pick all the dandelions and laugh the loudest.
Let them talk, and don't you listen.
You're a gem meant to shine,
too precious for words without compromise.
You'll never fit in and that's quite alright.
Diamonds are a treasure hidden out of sight.
If I could tell you everything I would say,
I'd fill the whole ocean and forever I'd stay.
I'd fight for a moment in time
When you could call me yours and I could call you mine.
I never imagined I'd forget your name—
Erased by darkness but you'll always remain—
A child of God, chosen and wanted—
I ache for the chance to tell you.
You are enough for all that you are.
If I could, I'd give you the stars.
I'd be the loudest out in the stands,
cheering past all life's demands.
I'd write a little note to declare
and tape it inside your lunch box with care.
You've got this, Elijah,
and please don't you forget that you are a diamond.
Treasure remains hidden until it's time to shine.

Shhhh...

I ALWAYS WANTED TO WRITE, but I didn't think it would be my story.
When I was a child, I was somewhat obsessed, okay, a lot obsessed,
with Martin Luther King Jr. More than his tenacity to stand against
oppression or embody love and grace in times of extreme hate, I
adored his voice because I really didn't have one. Yes, I was and

remain outspoken, but I was silent in the moments that mattered, the moments that shriek to remind me like nails on a chalkboard.

God convicts me many times over when it comes to the power of my tongue, often correcting what I've spoken, not what I've neglected to say. I can recall memories frozen in time like they were yesterday. My childhood replayed sounds of yelling and name-calling, doors slamming, and fists thrown. Behind closed doors, I remained silent. I was older than you, and I should've... I recall mental movie reels revealing what God asked me to do or say, but fear gripped me and my words grew hot as they climbed my throat and remained paralyzed on my tongue.

The juxtaposition between noise and silence in my life is quite baffling. From these lips of mine, I've praised God in church, leading worship, and cast down darkness behind closed doors, on my knees, crying waterfalls over those in my life. I've also submitted to long excruciating, complaining fits and gossiped about those I don't know. At times, I've used my tongue in wicked ways, as I'm sure you have too, but sometimes saying nothing is also a detriment.

Fear is an old trick cast by the enemy to cripple, and I'm finally recognizing the powerlessness in his tactics. Here's to speaking up, speaking out, and exposing the darkness to light. Let me be frank, my objective is not to shame or humiliate those who caused harm to my family. My objective is to show God strong through what the enemy tried to rob. Our enemies are not those in flesh in blood. In fact, we fight not against man but against principalities and powers. (Ephesians 6:12)

My shoes may be worn, but they've been reliable. Thank goodness God gave me a shiny new pair, and all I needed to do was recall who I was as I proclaim "There is no place like home in You."

The Gift of Peace

I'M IN A SPACE DESPERATE for grace, again.

I want to be held by a friend.
I do what I don't want to do—what I ache not to do.
My flesh often wins.
If I dig up the root, the lie that shows its face
is they've all abandoned, because you are replaced.
Is it something I lack?
Do I take up too much space?
Not enough, too much, certainly too far from grace.
A self-made island is what I call this place.
I take off my face another day
just a vice to consume all the noise in my head.
I'll lie down in bed—let out a great sigh.
I guess I'm alright.
If I dig up the root, the lie that shows its face
is they've all abandoned, because you are replaced.
I've traded tears and trust, hope and love for Mr. Right—
just another escape to smother my internal fight.
These memories flood through my mind,
pressing dams that crack with age.
They're ready to break.
Though I look in the mirror and I've removed my face,
it's not You, I see.
It's not Your grace.
I repeat this cycle until it breaks me.
One day, the truth I'll see.
Is it something I lack, do I take up too much space?
It feels like I'm being erased—like the error in his story—
head held high—he can walk in glory.
Two years have gone by, and this girl, I don't know her anymore.
My end goal, my finish line, what completes me is not a man.
It's not a child. It's not an external identity.
It's Him who made me.
"I do the thing I don't want to do."
Sounds like addiction.
We make our beds with the very demons we despise.

Without relinquishing the pain,
we relive the very thing we fear the most.
Suddenly, the emotionally absent parent
becomes the man in the mirror.
We revisit spaces like long-lost friends,
distant memories we'd catch for a glimpse of our end.
Fatality becomes a blanket, warm and inviting—
we'd rather sleep in.
The moment stretches and takes a new form,
a gripping reliance has been born.
Christmas comes with heavy pressures,
haphazard commitments, and surface reassurance.
I found this thing for you that shouts louder than
the inconceivable identity you formed for me, begging for mercy.
There are deep desires only God can fill and Santa can't deliver.
It can't be wrapped up or stuffed beneath a tree.
It's the gift of peace I really need.
When chaos rings like Christmas bells
and carols sound like reliving hell,
Won't it all come crashing down?
Hark, the herald angels sing!
Glory to the newborn King!
The gift has been delivered.
Will you open it?
The gift is within.

Humility or Humiliation?

I RECENTLY MET A JOLLY man who spoke of the difference between humiliation and humility. Near everyone around nodded in agreement as he informed us of the heart posture needed to be humble. I stewed and chewed on this and came to Jericho walls.

When we are safe, our walls dissipate. We let down the fortified walls meant for self-safety and let in the rains to cleanse us from the inside out. We are what we eat. If we stew on pain, our sight is colored by it. Everywhere we look, we see pain and relate it back to self.

The Hebrew word for *humility* is *Anah*, meaning oppressed. A test calls for a testimony. One who has been brought to the end of themselves has been fully emptied and can only be filled. So then, someone who has been emptied can only be filled unless they wallow in their oppressed form.

Oppression is to be wronged or exploited. Who can defend like the Father? Who can come against His throne?

He who accepts me accepts my Father. (Matthew 10:40) If God be for me, who can be against me? (Romans 8:31) The oil of joy is an exchange for mourning. (Isaiah 61:3)

Humility and humiliation are not the same. Nothing is wrong with humility. It doesn't convey the false narrative that you are weak or incapable. Yes, in our weakness, He is strong. Yes, we can only do all things in Christ. This humility to ask for help is strength. In the dumping of our cup, we are filled up by Him. He is our strength. Some of the strongest people I've met are believers. They are honest in their need of the Lord. They know that if it were up to them, they'd fumble the ball every time doing it alone.

There is no humiliation in asking. Ask Him. Lean on Him. The things we endure in this life are far too heavy for us to carry. You can't take those suitcases of burden with you. You must allow Him to carry them. He can shoulder anything. Nothing is too big for our God.

Are there things that come to mind
that you've carried for too long? Write what comes to mind.

_____

_____

_____

_____

_____

_____

Keep writing. Allow this space to dump from your heart
those things that have weighed you down.
It's alright to be vulnerable and real. Lay it down.

_____

_____

_____

_____

_____

_____

_____

_____

_____

_____

_____

_____

_____

———————

Guilty until Proven Innocent

HAVE YOU EVER FELT THE crack of a whip or smack on your rear for
something your sibling did? Have you stood in the corner ponder-
ing why everything is your fault? Our legal system is greatly flawed
and does not resemble "Innocent until proven guilty." The fast-paced
nuance of devices that allow for eyes on everyone at any time causes
internal scrutiny, debunking, and analyzing with every scroll, tap, or
like. The moment a thought is subjected to a different authority, the
game changes. Now, suddenly, we have run through the allegations
and pinned all the corresponding actions and reactions whether evidence or our own assumptions to the cross.

The enemy is an accuser. His goal is to rob, kill, and destroy.
He takes little truths and puts them under a microscope amplifying
them. Isn't this what court systems look like? Our courts do not
mimic the courts of heaven. We set someone on a pedestal and they

will surely fall every time. With all the eyes on them, waiting for a wrong move, listing out every wrong, and filling in the gaps of misunderstanding, the accused begins to fall trap to the lies, who the accuser says they are.

This is a mental picture of what Satan seeks to do to us. It's vital we know who we are. When we know who we are and whose we are, we won't let the oil in our lamps go out, always relying on the oil supply. Rather than rely on our own strength that instantly runs dry, we fall into His divine strength. His supply is endless, a grace that helps to uphold us when all the dark seems to swallow us up. We will let our lights shine. This flickering flame will become a blazing fire.

"But He was wounded for our transgressions, He was bruised for our iniquities; the chastisement for our peace was upon Him, and by His stripes we are healed." (Isaiah 53:5)

We are not under the old covenant to slaughter animals and shed blood for our transgressions. In fact, it has all been paid for. When accusation comes knocking, remind yourself of what the truth is. We all fall short, but nothing external can define who we are.

We are all like the lost sheep that fall into the snare, into the pit over and over again, but He leaves the ninety-nine for the one. The ninety-nine have each other. The one is isolated by the lie to take it out.

"Be sober, be vigilant; because your adversary the devil walks about like a roaring lion, seeking whom he may devour." (1 Peter 5:8) Isolation kills. The lion waits for the gazelle to leave the group to attack. He swoons your mind with lies—you don't have a seat at the table, they don't understand—or he will remind you of the comforting presence of pain. Be so comfortable with freedom that you never desire to go back into hiding, into shame, into the lie that pain is comfortable. Familiar is fruitless. To grow, a plant has to be plucked of the dead stuff. We must be willing to grow and not let the dead stuff of what is temporary or past burn out our light. He desires to do a new thing. Do you perceive it?

Follow His voice. His sheep know His voice. He always makes a way of escape for you. Are you listening?

"No temptation has overtaken you expect such as is common to man; but God is faithful, who will not allow you to be tempted beyond what you are able, but with the temptation will also make the way of escape, that you may be able to bear it." (1 Corinthians 10:13) He is the way of escape. What is the lie that has you searching for truth at the bottom of a liquor bottle or in the arms of a paid-for woman? What is the lie that holds you in bondage? The truth will make you free and the only thing that opposes the truth is a lie. What are the lies? Those are the hidden things that God exposes with His light to make you righteous, to be made right, by truth. Our courts need a facelift. God's law is grace, and He has made you new. "For He made Him who knew no sin to be sin for us, that we might become the righteousness of God in Him." (2 Corinthians 5:21)

What Would You Say?

IF I COULD GO BACK in time to visit my younger self, I would tell her a thing or two. But first, I would hug her. She never received enough affection—just lip service, rejection, false promises, and comprise always on her end.

I would sit her down and make her believe that she is worthy of love, that she is impossibly strong and that she is one of the best friends she has yet to have herself. I would let her curls down from that pinned-back bun she always wears to contain what she thought was a rat's nest—that's what they called it. I would twirl each one in my fingers and look her in the eyes with the slight crease of a smile to show her that she wasn't quite invisible.

We would go on an adventure through the future while I held her hands and let her see into my gaze—the fight, the purpose, the freedom, and even the rage. She would cry as she watched the memories fall apart, and then she'd laugh, all the feels of a perfectly good Hallmark movie.

But in the end, I'd remove my hands from hers, returning her gaze, and I'd say, "It's okay to not be enough. It's okay to not feel okay. But, don't stay there too long. Those feelings are like a monster with an insatiable appetite, taking the host for the ride of a lifetime. Take time to breathe in every good thing, every belly laugh, every trouble-making innocent deed, all the bedroom dance parties and sleepovers, take all of it in every chance you get. Don't take one breath for granted. And then exhale the exhaustion, the burdens that aren't yours to carry, the lies you tell yourself to get rest, the "have to be better to feel loved" lies. Just let it all out, and don't breathe it back in. You only have today once. You won't get to see it again. The moments can't be relived or experienced. In your mind's eye, piecing all the moving fragments together, lean in, take a leap, and don't worry about the fall. You have a Father who will always catch you. Let that be enough. He is enough."

I would bid her farewell and remind her to lift her head, fix her crown, and face each day with gratitude in her heart, grace in her footsteps, and hope for tomorrow.

If you could speak to your younger self, what would you say?

_____

_____

_____

_____

_____

_____

_____

_____

—————————————

You Are Mine!

If I COULD SAY IT all this time,
I'd take the clock and rewind.
To a time when I knew your face.

I'd like to go back to those days, revisit a space in time.
When all I had was laundry piles and you on my mind.
Such a tender loving child.
You were brave and you were wild.
Nothing kept your words at bay.
I'd really love to keep it that way.
You were a dandelion. Wild and free.
A little unknown, a little part of me.
But somehow you've gone away,
a part of me died that day.
Although I have a piece of you
I've kept in my pocket for the days I feel blue,
I can't help but plead for the wind to bring you back to me.
Bring me back to bedtime stories,
tear-filled eyes when I kissed you goodnight,
knowing one day you'll grow up tall,
dodging my kisses like a fastball.
Bring me your hugs to warm the night
when all feels desperately lonely and I'm not alright
thinking about losing what was most precious to me,
my child of God I no longer see.
I can't paint a silver lining on a cloud that bares no sun
for it was never in God's plan to see a family undone.
I've tucked away my prayers for a faith I couldn't hold
until something shifted and my prayers became bold.
Shame was an enemy I kept at my door,
fearing my truth and all that it stands for.
But I've since kicked him out.
His presence became a burden and my heart has had enough.
I looked him in the face and called his bluff.
Prayer looks like war and I'm fit for battle.
This mountain in my way I'm ready to tackle!

PART SIX

DELIVERANCE

"Nothing comes to a sleeper but a dream."
Serena Williams

Delivered from the Lie

COMPARE AN OUTER SHELL TO our giving birth. We must birth these things. We've prepared for it though we cannot see what is coming. We have faith. We celebrate, and all bring gifts in faith for what is to come. We pray for what's inside to be healthy and whole, unhindered. Our outer shell is our skin protecting our organs. God made our bodies to defend, and our minds are defended by the word.

Deliverance—delivering happens by way of speaking the truth! "And you shall know the truth, and the truth shall make you free." (John 8:32)

What lies are you holding on to keeping you from that birth?

_____

_____

_____

_____

_____

_____

You Can Do It, Mama!

I REMEMBER WHEN I HAD my daughter Neya. I was so scared that she wouldn't love me because I held to the lie that my mom didn't love me. It wasn't true of course, but I held it closely anyway. I made friends with this lie so much that, when it came time to push, I shook with a great anxiety, panicking with my legs in stirrups, and crying out that surely she wouldn't love me.

I had one nurse who spoke sharply with me, and it only made it worse. (You catch more flies with honey.) Then the doctor spoke to me. He spoke kindly and reminded me of the past when I had birthed two other healthy babies who love me. (The word is like honey to our lips.) Suddenly I was able to push because my focus became Jesus. I remember looking up and seeing what I believe to be God or an angel, a great light. I can't really recall it, but it wasn't the birthing lights. This light and those words guided me home. I kept telling myself I could do this, recounting all the women who had done so before me and drawing on the memories I had stored up with Elijah and Tristen.

I pushed and pushed, and finally, Neya was born. Neya Elizabeth. Her name means Light of God. This child defeated the lie that my daughter wouldn't love me. When I sang to her as a little two-year-old (and even now), she looked at me with the most tender, adoring eyes. I look back at videos from a recent birthday party with Emerson and from one when Neya was two, and I am honored that she looks at me with love.

Push! This is what it means to break through. A test is part of the testimony. It was never meant to kill you, only to crush you and produce oil. That oil can be used on and for EVERYTHING. It is meant to awaken someone else.

Let God crack you open, break through those lies, deliver what's inside from what looks ugly. What's being delivered looks more beautiful than you could ever know. Give Him a try. Trust Him.

Who knows the creation better than the Creator? Who knows what to do better than the One who made the instruction manual?

Be delivered.

Came up Clean

I'VE SAT IN A STEAMING bath as the dirt settled and looked me right in the eyes. The salt from my gaze fell like waterfalls from my cheeks to drench me in release. I've felt the heart cry for my enemies, of those never meant to stand against me, but meant to be a ministry. I've ached for righteousness in the face of evil to be undone by perfect love, cast into a sea of blood and forgiveness. Brother, you may not break me, but I'll help you heal your broken glass. I want to be who the Lord made me, so I'll soak up these tears knowing they reflect a heart of love pleading for those who have hurt me. My body will change, my heart be reconciled, and my mind be made new. I am not my own, and for this, I find you in a dirty bubble bath.

Everything in this world is meant to serve the Lord—even the ugly bits. He works ALL things together, right? The Word tells us to bless those who curse us and to pray for those who spitefully use us. It goes as far as saying to love our enemies. (Luke 6: 27–28) If we are honest, this Scripture has not always sat well with us. Maybe we feel justified by having walls of protection up against those who have done us dirty. If God uses all these things to "work together for good to those who love God, to those who are the called according to His purpose," then He has plans to use all the things. (Romans 8:28) Sometimes the very things sent to destroy you will actually mature you. Sometimes the things that took from you actually gave to you.

I didn't truly know the love of God, being seen by God, until I lost everything. Sure, the Scripture says, "oil of joy for mourning," and it was made alive in my life. I was dumped of self, and though I'll never agree with those who did me and my family dirty, I know that God uses all things. He has and will continue to.

"To console those who mourn in Zion, to give them beauty for ashes, the oil of joy for mourning, the garment of praise for the spirit of heaviness; that they may be called trees of righteousness, the planting of the Lord, that He may be glorified." (Isaiah 61:3)

To have true and lasting joy after great mourning is rare, but it doesn't have to be. We don't have to be governed by our emotions, circumstances, or past experiences. We can choose joy. Righteousness is to be made right, to be planted in the Lord with right standing in identity. That is lasting and brings Him glory. How else would someone have a smile on their face if not for the Lord? How else is a person pulled from the pits of depression, suicide, drug or alcohol addiction, pornography, or anything of this world that seeks to take our souls and make itself Lord over our lives? Jesus used the least of these, the castaways of society, to minister to others' freedom. Why? Who else is a better candidate than one who has left their old life behind to start anew? He who loses life can only gain it back.

"He who loves his life will lose it, and he who hates his life in this world will keep it for eternal life." (John 12:25)

A cup that has been emptied can only be filled. When we are full of ourselves, be it pain or pride, we cannot be filled with the Lord. We cannot serve Him and ourselves nor two masters. If we return back to the notion of our enemies, we must understand that as we have been given grace, we must give it. We have been given love, and we must give it. This life of righteousness is not meant to hoard the love, joy, and peace we have but to act as a lighthouse guiding others home. Loving Judas in our lives is a good test of what we really believe. It's easy to love and accept Jesus, but those who hurt us challenge what we have our faith in. And I know, well I don't know you specifically, but I have known a great deal of pain from those who have misused me, slandered me, put their hands on me, abandoned and abused me, but God. It's always but God. Your enemies are not flesh and blood. Those individuals are God's children too. Did Jesus not also die for them to have perfect union with Him as well? Let our hearts not be divided with justification in our own pain and anger toward others while praising with our tongues in another moment. This is what it means to be double-minded, and most of my life I had been just that.

Baptism is a symbol of what it means to go down dirty and come up clean, but I'm not talking about behavior modification. I'm not talking about sin modification. I'm talking about an upheaval of the lies and roots that cause the behavior. If you keep pulling the leaves off a weed without pulling the root, you'll keep getting that same nasty thing in your garden. It can also take over and choke out the good things you've planted and taken care to nourish. Let God make you clean by visiting the untouchable places in your heart and mind, those riddled with pain—those you have barred up with walls of self-protection. He is your fortress. Let Him take a look at that splinter and gently pull it up.

Splish-splash, you'll be taking a bath.

Over and Over

OUR MINDS ARE BATTLEFIELDS LIKE boxing rings, and trauma will drag you into the ring again and again if you allow it. I find myself in a tormenting cycle, replaying the voices of my enemies. I could've done something different. If I would've spoken up or stayed silent. If I would have lied. If I would have given up. If I were to say something different.

Satan is the master tormentor. I don't say that to boast in his power. He is ultimately defeated, and we must believe that and stand firm in who God says we are. I've not mastered it all, but I'm sharing through my learning. Nothing is more humbling than to let others inside to see the shattered pieces, all the reflections and versions of you that you'd rather conceal. Here I am three minutes into typing this on my iPhone, and I realize that "Over and Over" is playing on Spotify.

How does God speak to you?

_____
_____
_____
_____
_____
_____

Hindsight 20/20

TODAY WAS A COMPILING OF a few stand-out messages from 2020 as Pastor Steven Fertick's wife, Holly Fertick, put it "Trace the favor of God through all of it." Four messages were highlighted—"Make Room for the New," "Tired on the Inside," "Unschedulable Blessings," and "Did I Ask?" A reel was played from each message throughout the year starting nine months ago.

The first one highlighted a statement—"He is going to use people you don't even like to grow you up and mature you." Looking back, I had every inclination that the woman caring for my daughters would have to be a monster to have gone along with the lies told to her. I never imagined most of those lies remained in the courts to serve the state's purpose rather than revealed to all. I imagined that my daughters would not grow to know they were adopted or know anything about me. I thought it would be years before being reunited. I built up a dislike for who I thought this woman was. She has taught me what being obedient to God looks like and what being humble and tender-hearted looks like.

The next message showed that while Jesus was the Son of God and without blemish, He maintained the tiresome woes of man. He was not without exhaustion. Pastor identified the way he feels when he gets tired and stretched too thin—angry. He sounds like me. I become angry with myself, like I don't have enough strength in my own efforts. Sometimes I push until I break rather than sitting in God's peace when needed and going to the source of peace and comfort. Pastor said that, when we get tired, often we begin fighting everything, including battles that don't matter to distract from those that actually do. This couldn't be more true. I often allow myself to become balled up with small frustrations, projecting the larger pains that I stray from dealing with or rather allowing God to deal with.

The last two messages were powerful. Speaking on God's schedule was convicting at the moment. Looking back, I am grateful God does what He is going to do in His time. My timing looked like meeting my daughters after they were over twelve years old, when they had decided who I was and everything about me, and when they had discovered they were adopted and out of curiosity reached out only to discover how broken I was. I assumed I would be broken or that somehow I'd let them down. Fertick said that God could bless us ahead of schedule and that "some of the best things happen apart from your schedule." My best things started with a phone call as I went to clock in at work. I almost ignored the call as I was preparing for work, but I knew my sister wouldn't ordinarily call knowing that I was working. In His timing, God showed me that day what His love looked like and began laying the groundwork to unite and bless the way He had been showing me in dreams.

The final message was called "Did I ask?" The enemy placed condemnation in nearly every area of my life, as a mother and a wife, as a daughter and as a woman. Rather than asking God, the ultimate authority in my heart, I took to heart words spoken over me about who I was as a woman, a wife, a daughter, and a mother. Those words robbed who God said I was. This message began to tug at those false words. I remember listening to this message sobbing and wrestling with who God said I was and what "authority figures" said I was. The enemy planted examples in my mind of my children being taken and that being evidence of being a crappy mother. He used words of mockery and judgment from my family and the courts when I remained in my marriage after finding out about the adultery and trying to seek counsel. I replayed every condemning word about what a selfish daughter I was not to call my family or find out what was going on in their lives while everything I loved was stolen out of my arms.

But *God* said...This was the foundation. I assumed I was not enough because of what everyone else said. I kept telling God who I was, as determined by all authorities that had no ultimate authority in my life or in my spirit. Fertick added that God would put something in you for the right timing. If He asks something of you, He gave you enough in preparation to do the thing He asked. Pastor gave his son his wallet before the sermon and called him up on stage, asking for a particular amount of cash. The boy recalled the wallet his dad gave him. God gave me Emerson. God sowed these words in my heart to begin reshaping the way He saw me and show me who He was!

Holly Fertick noted that God gives you all that you need for what He is calling you to do. Today, I have rights to my son. The courts are no longer in my life. I have the documentation and legal authority to have my child, dismantling the lies of the enemy and causing doubt in what Ohio deemed, in all their rational, to take my children. As I reflect on 2020, the year truly was a year of favor. I couldn't always see it, and it was painful and isolating at times, but I can now see all the ways God was speaking to me and moving. More than anything, God has reshaped what I saw in Him.

Throughout the case, losing my children, and having to move to Washington to fight for my child, I had conceptions of God that were wrong. I started to deny my faith and began believing that God was not real, not capable, and as powerless as I. He showed me He was my and everyone else's authority. He is stronger, He is capable, He is enough, He is alive and real, He is accessible, and He is love. I know that every year will be even better because God has given me spiritual eyes to see the ways he was working in 2020 to build my faith in His love, His goodness, His authority, and His ability. If my God be for me, whom shall I fear?

This piece was written on January 3, 2021. Now we are in 2024, and I am blown away by the growth. Habbakuk 2:2–3 is such an important verse to me, so important that I had it tattooed on my right hand to remind me every time I wrote.

"Then the Lord answered me and said: 'Write the vision and make it plain on tablets, that he may run who reads it. For the vision is yet for an appointed time; but at the end it will speak, and it will not lie…" (Habbakuk 2:2–3)

Writing it all down is important. Why is the Bible so powerful? Why is it such a source for us? Because, someone, many someones decided to write it down. We need to heed His Word because it is a light to our path. When things get dark, we use our flashlight, the Word. We can test this life with the Word—What does God say about it? When God speaks, write it down! When you are learning in a classroom setting, you take notes because they are important for the upcoming test. Life is exactly the same way. We need the words of the Lord.

Write it all down. Then, when you get discouraged, revisit how God worked in your life. You will see the growth in your person over the years. We read directions to make something and to go somewhere. Why are we not jotting down what God says? One of the most powerful tools we have is a pen. It gives a voice to what's inside. I've collected five to seven journals of writing from the last seven years. If I had been more consistent, the writing would have been all in one place as the last four have been. Much of this book contains writings from those journals.

Have you ever heard the saying, "The pen is mightier than the sword?" Now you have. The Word of God is compared to a sword and it's a collection of penmanship. Don't find yourself contemplating hindsight. Write it. Write it all down.

Winston Churchill says it best—"History is written by the victors." You have the victory in Christ. Tell your story for the enemy is overcome by "the blood of the Lamb and the word of our testimonies." (Revelation 12:11)

He Sees You

I SEE YOU THERE, RATTED hair with lips pressed up against a bottle. Did it again, let sin creep its way in. Finding it hard to forgive yourself. What if I told you I know a man whose fountains never run dry, whose love will tenderly dry those eyes, who will fight for you the way your mama didn't, and who will stand up when he let it happen? Trade your drink, and you will thirst no more. Seek your Creator, our Lord. He dearly loves you.

Tales They Tell

EACH COURTROOM VISIT WAS LIKE an interrogation. Being painted into a corner became increasingly uncomfortable. Gossip is a whisper that dances through corridors, a cackle in a beauty shop, and a bold lie in a courtroom. A sort of boldness is in an unapologetic, unaccountable lie. It's blackened with sin, but no one sees her stripes. I suppose our America can relate to sin that started with a whisper, fueled by hate now a blaze with streets on fire.

Who are these liars? They're the "it's okay" and "this one time won't hurt" white lies we tell ourselves. They look like poking fun or assuming stories in our minds. Until one day, our words have slain another, all they've held dear gone, in a courtroom, families ripped apart, and suicide in a headline. When you think of the deadliest sin, I'm sure murder comes to mind, but isn't something more terrifying when it's cloaked and in disguise? A bear could mull and kill. A lion too. What's worse is a monster appearing as a friend, who gains your trust and thirsts for blood in the end.

I've learned what it means to love your enemies and to bless those who curse you. What a heresy this used to feel like. How could I observe someone with loving eyes who did me so dirty? I'll tell you. When you spend time with Jesus, you look more like Him, and your lens changes. Jesus knew that Judas would betray Him, yet He sat and broke bread with Judas at the Last Supper before being crucified. Who is your Judas? I won't lie to you—at first, it feels foreign and uncomfortable. With time, your heart softens, and God changes your lens to see everyone in a new light. No longer do you desire vengeance, but justice remains. *Justice* is closely aligned with the word *righteousness*, meaning "to make right." If Jesus died for all, He isn't coming for your enemies' heads, is He? Correction and love are reflections of a good parent, just like the Lord, but this fire-and-brimstone God was put away when blood was shed for ALL. I didn't stutter. All. This excerpt is important because I need you to drink in the pain in those words. I'm not unfamiliar. My pain is relatable in and through all the tests I've needed to endure. To come out the other side, changed, is a testimony to God's love and faithfulness—to everything He is. His desire is that we have peace with all men if possible.

"If it is possible, as much as depends on you, live peaceably with all men." (Romans 12:18) "Blessed are the peacemakers, for they shall be called sons of God." (Matthew 5:9)

Loving your enemy and forgiving is as much about them as it is about you. What happens when you don't forgive? You put a barrier around that part of your heart. Now you've hardened yourself, and your own unforgiveness walls you away from experiencing freedom. What if, instead of desiring payback for that person, you desire freedom? No matter who you are, your broken pieces cut those in your path—be it your friends or loved ones. We have all hurt someone with unhealed parts of ourselves. Self sabotage. Our enemy is but one, and he was already defeated. The only wrestling we do is in our mind, and even that, we have the tools to conquer.

I know a guy, and He says, "We are more than conquerors through Him who loved us." (Romans 8:31–39)

Doubt Not Unbelief

WHEN DOUBT LOOKS LIKE I'VE failed you, I guess I never could be.
The one you anointed and called, You said that I had victory.
Every mountain I face and valley I've made it through,
You've never failed me.
It's all because of You.
I can't earn Your love; Your grace is like an ocean.
When I'm fighting faith, Your love sets me in motion.
To move, to speak, to love, to lead—it all starts with humility.
The truth is, I'll fail a thousand times again
and still You call me friend.
When it looks like doubt, You've got me somehow.
It's not over, and You're not done—
guess I'm used to being not enough for everyone.
But You're strong in my weakness—Y
our love is relentless.
I'm undone at the ways You love me.
I fight and I war, internal I'm torn,
and all the while You're waiting.

You know this heart of mine,
I'm breaking while I say that I'm fine.
I believe.
Help me dismantle my unbelief.

Mama

I'M NOT JUST LIKE YOU. I have pains you see right through. Hyper-aware, standing on the edge. There is more than simply stress. My heart jumps at adventure as my child takes risks. His desire to grow is held at bay while I assess risk. He wants to leap, and I wait for his fall. I'm shaking inside, feeling so small. When I talk about fear, it's not simply a notion or even a meltdown that causes commotion. I'm hyperaware of every heartache. All the things that keep me awake. I'm aware of his pain and his need for love. I'm afraid of all the things he does.

When did going to the park induce a panic attack? What happens if he falls down and gets cracked? Humpty Dumpty couldn't have had a more helicopter mother, but if I don't hover, who will be there to smother? Who will be there to ensure that he stays safe? Who will guard his need for thrill, making sure he does turn out like Jack and Jill? Was there anyone looking for their parents at a simple mistake? This tightrope is too much to take! I'm a mama just like you, but the loss I've endured not many could see through. Some days are hard, and some moments are like boulders, but I wish with all my heart this pain would soon be over.

I can recall going to a park in Washington with a friend of mine, my son Emerson, and her little girl who was practically the same age. My son in all his bravery, his name literally meaning "brave," would jump and scuttle in a race with the wind to see how quickly he could maneuver across playscapes. It was like the old adage that "if you step on a crack, you break your mother's back." Ahhh. I couldn't even let out a breath because, surely if he fell, who would believe me when I took him to the hospital? There we were in the brisk Pacific air, and while my friend joyfully watched her daughter, I held my breath and waited to jolt into action at the slightest misstep. Luckily, I could feel what was happening and opened up to my friend as I couldn't bear a moment more with my mind and body stiffened in submission to anxiety. She looked at me with such hope and assurance and reminded me that I wasn't in Ohio. I was in Washington. She reminded me that I had my son and all else was noise, essentially. I let out a sigh of relief and tried to find enjoyment in a simple play without fear.

Mama, you'll never do anything perfectly. God never expected perfection, people did. You are the woman for the job. God knew just what your child needed and what you needed. He made those hearts of yours, and no one can do it like you. It's not the external stuff that matters. It's the filling inside. You are not a carbon copy of anyone. Each of us has contradictions to walk through as parents. He prepares us for what He has for us, and that preparation is made available by following His lead. We never had to be perfect.

I used to be *that* mom—you know, the Pinterest one. I once spent eleven hours making a pirate ship cake for my oldest son's birthday. I used to sit with my kiddo who had an upcoming birthday and allow them to choose a theme and then a few cakes they liked. I'd select the one I thought I could accomplish and go for it. The making of that cake revealed my heart posture. I would push and push to ensure every detail was perfect so they would know without a single doubt how loved they were. That was a picture of fear.

It's great to desire our kiddos to know we love them and to do things to showcase it, but when we start striving for perfection, we miss the point. Sure the party would go off without a hitch, but I always had so much pressure internally to make sure it was all perfect.

Mama, breathe. The dishes can wait. The floors riddled with crumbs will be there tomorrow, but those cuddles don't last forever. You'll never have this moment again. Take joy and delight in each and every one. See them as God does. Don't make them an idol, but know that this child is a unique expression of God. He formed their tiny toes and belly laughs. He knew the thing that would fuel their desires and aches. And you, Mama, are a gift to them as much as they are to you. Make sure you know the Giver, not just the gift. One day, that gift grows up, makes their own choices, and lives their own life, but you don't have to be an empty nester. You know the Giver. Take comfort knowing that they too hear from God.

If you are a mama or if you struggle with perfecting things, what do you think the root cause is?
Is there a lie that needs to be exposed and canceled by truth?

_____

_____

_____

_____

_____

_____

_____

Take Inventory

TAKE INVENTORY ON ALL THE thoughts you've allowed yourself to believe. What are they?

- Something is lacking in me. I'm not pretty enough, talented enough, strong enough, smart enough, well enough equipped.
- Nothing will ever change. Your kids don't know you, nor do they care to.
- You are only worth what you can give. If you can't give, you are not useful.
- No one wants you. You are not worth anything.

These are thoughts that took root because I took the bait (lie) and ran with it. I let the seed settle, work, and take root. Like a fish who takes food off a hook, a lie will latch itself to you and take you for a ride to the depths of despair—if you allow it.

After you've taken inventory of all the negative thoughts you've latched on to, all the lies that are not from God, replace them. Begin uprooting them with truth, and rewire your mind.

First, understand that He is the only one who can dictate who you are and your worth. He made you, and only the creator knows the value of its creation. God says that I'm enough; in fact, I'm more than enough because He has good plans for my future. He loves me and chose me; I wasn't an accident. God is an intentional God who designed my unique heart and mind for purposes beyond my understanding. God works all things for the good of those who love Him. I am family. He doesn't walk away when I act out or speak out of line. He doesn't call me dramatic or too much. He speaks to me tenderly in whispers I can hear when I silence myself. He corrects and protects me for He has better.

Take inventory of your thoughts below.
List the lies, and on the next page, list the truths (combative Scriptures). Allow the Lord to help you sort out where those lies started so you can heal the source. "And you shall know the truth, and the truth shall make you free." (John 8:32)

Lies
Example: I am not good enough.

_____

_____

_____

_____

_____

_____

_____

_____

_____

_____

_____

Truth

Example: "I will praise You,
for I am fearfully and wonderfully made;
marvelous are Your works, and that my soul knows very well."
(Psalm 139:14)

My Lighthouse

I was drowning in the wreckage, unsure that You'd find me, causing waves of anxiety to swallow up the best parts of me.

And I just knew that You wouldn't want me after all I did and all I said. Who I was when I thought You couldn't see me.

But in the storm, You met me, waves crashed all around Your feet, and You embraced all my ugly—all the hidden things I found myself buried beneath.

You found me.

They say I've gotta work harder and I look stronger when I stand like that. But I know I'm really breaking underneath these shallow walls I've built around me.

They say, I've gotta smile big enough to chase my pain away, but I don't quite feel like it these days.

Drowning is survival at its best, anything to keep me afloat, dragging chaos out of peace to find a false rest.

But You're my lighthouse. You guide me home. You fill all my broken places with light—I know I'm going to be alright when You shine through the night.

Take my heart. I won't be afraid. I'll follow after You. With eyes on my lighthouse, I have faith to move.

(Matthew 14:2–33)

Home Is with You

I MISS HOME, BUT I don't know where that is—too much chasing time lost and trying to fit in. Will all of these things I do make a difference—all of the hours I've spent living life vicarious? This life has me jumping through hoops—if I only try hard enough, I'll start to look more like you. The more I try to fit my square in a round hole, the more you tell me that's not how I made you. I made you for more than sitting on the sidelines, watching laughter fly by just out of reach. You were made to change the room—set it on fire like I do in you. Stop chasing and running, I made you for rest—even the birds have no one to impress. Your home is with Me, wherever you go and whoever you see. You'll take me with you as with your breath. Home is everywhere between this world and the next.

It helps to take the thoughts you are feeling and dump them on a page. They don't have to sound pretty or make any sense at all, but freedom is in releasing the very words you play on repeat. Seeing them on a page makes them real. What am I really believing? Have you ever said something and realized just how silly it was? Taking inventory in that moment, our feelings become irrational, and the words out of our mouth give revelation to such powerlessness as empty words. This is often how God speaks to me. I'll begin writing all the irrational nonsense taking up space in my mind and then there is a reply, truth to combat the lies.

―――――――

Punching Bag

I WAS FINE UNTIL I wasn't. It took falling on my face to feel the sting of needing grace. And when I fell, something broke loose and I could feel again. I'm not okay with being a punching bag but more so having my children knocked around. All of my children were rehomed and renamed like animals—like their identity was ripped away before the seed could take root. I want to be at peace, and the more my life rolls on, the better suited for the theater I become. I think I've taken this character too seriously. Instead of releasing pain, I store it up, inhale, and let it grow. It feels like a cancer, but I don't let it show. No one knows.

I had a dream so real I felt like I could reach out and grab it. My girls were full of excitement as they pulled me into all their favorite places in their house, introducing me to siblings and their rooms. And then my oldest daughter wanted me to stay for Christmas, but the bittersweet has become tart at the cost of robbing memories and taking scraps of what was mine. I sit on the sidelines and watch her raise my girls, and she does so well.

Some days I'm the woman God made me, and others I'm fighting to keep my head above water. How does a mother window shop her own children, watching their lives like Disney shorts—only a teaser to show you what you're missing and what you can't take home? Even after God moved again and again, confirming the parallel heart cry also within my daughters, it slipped through my fingers and I left again with a measly goodbye as they drove off, not knowing when I'd see them again and who they would be next time. Sometimes I feel frozen in pain while everyone else is in fast forward journeying through life as I watch mine slip away. I'm so tired. I can't take another hit, and I have no defense to protect my babies. A mother's worst fear is their child going through pain, fear, sickness, and not being able to do a thing about it, and I've been stuck on the sidelines of this sick movie reel for way too long. I'm not even part of the show with my sons.

This piece was written in January 2022, and I still feel these things. However, while it still hurts and remains wildly unjust and cruel, I don't stay in those emotions. I process through them and not let them drive the bus of my day or my identity. My reality doesn't even dictate who I am and who God is. This faith walk has been nothing short of wild, but His fingerprints are on everything. I don't have to be a punching bag for my emotions or my reality. I can rest knowing that He is good no matter what. His goodness and His character don't change. Just because a person does you dirty doesn't mean God approves of it. Quit taking punches from the enemy. Hand over your gloves and rest.

Running Ahead

IF MY PAIN RUNS AHEAD of me, my tongue slays those who beseech me to be still, silent. My shame, she teases me, whispering petty lies to stumble my feet into snares that would easily swallow me whole. All of this life deduced to words spoken out of tune, a key that no one comprehends but my own pain. She is fueled by the incessant need to be heard. She laughs with every swing of my sword. Though I've traded in weaponry and sought after a blade that cuts with truth, that defends its own without offense and defense birthed from fight or flight—sometimes I slip into the old man, familiar spirits. Pain, she is a liar. She'll coax you with memories of things otherwise forgotten. She thrusts me into thoughts that are not my own. It's alright, darling, remember this is not your home. But this mental anguish has to end. It's not all that familiar; it's not my friend. Its cause is for you to confess—pinned up against duress. You'll agree with these lies that I've laid out for you. You'll put on this garment and refuse truth. Just defend your own, and they'll all see what you believe.

Lies! I call down everything that seeks to exalt itself, boasting against the truth. He is the way, the truth, and the light. I am His daughter, and He puts up the fight. I'll surrender this rudder that once steered my ship. There's a new captain aboard—lay hold of my lips. I'll speak the promises You laid before the foundation of time. I can't say that this form I have is mine. Your weapons are ancient, and history proves it. Nothing is standing in Your way—nothing You won't move. I submit to You my pain, this thorn in my paw. This life was never mine at all. (James 3:4–6; Psalm 52:5–7; Ephesians 6:11–13)

Dancing in the Rain

I WAKE WITH CRIES IN my heart, imagining that it's you all alone in the dark, but maybe it's me who can't help but hurt from the endless memories I play on repeat. Maybe your joy can't be contained, and all of the beauty that was once rain is the image of God on display for all to see. I can't help but wonder if you think of me.

Do you recall the time we had—the ways I comforted you when you were sad. The praying away every fear that took hold as you laid down your head. The dancing parties in the living room, the way we would shake out our feelings like Boom! BOom! BOOm! The speakers would dance along with us, and oh, the laughter that sprung from the kitchen while my inner child joined in—not a care in the world—our hair twirled in the wind.

Do you remember? I'll choose to see a child drenched in love though it's not mine to give. I'll choose to reassign the pain to myself because I couldn't bear you to carry it. Don't let the world stomp out your peace and joy. Dance in the rain!

Rooted

THE WORDS "SUFFER WELL" PLAY on repeat in my mind. Even if I suffer in knowing You'll deliver on Your Word—that it returns with it a promise so pure and beautiful it exceeds my aches—I still want. When God? It's been too long.

I imagine my sons have traded in cuddles for time alone, every moment with mama for scrolling on a phone. I can't seep into the ignorance that suddenly my children will return from whence they came, toddling with echoes of "I love you" on their lips, silly rhymes, and finger-holding grip.

How can you reverse the damage that's been done to my only sons? My little girls' dresses that twirl, ribbons and curls. This word doesn't feel alive to me. It feels like an ache I've spent too long in a state of plea. Why God? When God? Why not me?

If Your promise is heritage, a natural gift, why do I have to wait for justice delivered and return on what was taken? This confusion often leaves me stolen in statue form, no thought of cause or action. What can I do but wait?

I don't feel I have a choice. I'm like Ariel, robbed of my voice. How do I live in the present today? Let today be a gift like I didn't lose all my yesterdays. I trust that You're good, but Your hand feels harsh.

Sometimes I feel so small, like I've died and in a moment everyone moved on. It's old news to think of what was done, like a murder never figured out, case closed. No one to scream or shout. Just a girl, a little lost, faded into the background. How do you miss a voice that was never heard? Her eyes plead for a new tomorrow. Don't let her die on this hill. She's been climbing for too long.

I've learned that this desperation is caused by making the test my identity. I trust Him less for the testimony to be birthed as beauty from ashes. I question how, when, and why? I've filled in the blanks of my mind. Isn't this how we play God? I don't know all the whys. I can't control what is out of my reach, but I can know the gift-giver and not replace it with the gift. We can want so much that the want takes center stage. In the barrenness, I've been filled with rivers of living water—joy that seems impossible. I can have the things He promised me—a sound mind, mourning to joy, beauty from ashes, praise instead of heaviness. I've had to ask myself the hard question. What if it doesn't happen? What if my children don't care to know the truth? Is God still good?

The truth is that He doesn't change. The things around us happen, and we can allow them to change our identity or we can be rooted.

What is external to you does not define you. Stop allowing it to. What happened to you or for you—even by you—is not who you are. *Identity* is defined as "this" in Hebrew. We look at a thing and name it to define it. This is _____ . If we are a new creation, then this is what God says it is, period. It is named by God, and nothing external can define its identity. I am as He says.

I've allowed external experiences to define who I am for too long. I told myself that I am not a mother because of what others said of me and have done to me. I told myself I was unworthy of love because of how I allowed men to treat me. But God. He says that I am a mother to many, no matter how I think it should look. The test, the contradiction, reveals what our faith is in. He says I was created to be a helper to my husband. I don't have to become the identity He says I am. I just need to believe that what He made is good.

He who is trusted with little can be trusted with much. (Luke 16:10) If you cannot stand firm in who you are now, how can you expect to maintain the identity when you have what you've asked for? If you believe you are poor, you'll begin to look like what you believe. You will spend all you are given because you identify with "poor." Did you know the vast majority of lottery winners go broke after winning such large sums of money? Why do you think that is? If you believe you are not enough, you'll become like it. So a man thinks he is. (Proverbs 23:7)

I remember being in a college course called "Gender, Role, and Identity" some ten years ago, when the Lord started to connect the dots between psychology and the Word of God concerning our identity. This same verse about thinking and becoming is also "Self-fulfilling Prophecy" in psychology. It's wild to think how much He revealed to me over the years, especially in college where nearly every single paper I wrote came down to identity, but it didn't sink in. Even in high school, the Lord spoke to me. God is always speaking, and sometimes we forget how much He has spoken until He lifts the veil and we go back and revisit all the ways He was there. We enlivened the lie that this was a first introduction, but it wasn't. He makes known all the times He was there. We aren't ever abandoned.

Back on topic. Believing you are not enough and self-sabotaging becomes the expression of what you believe. The relationship dissolves at the hands of your own lies, previous experience, or emotions. Looking in the rearview of experience directs your path right into a ditch. If you believe, it is made evident by how you walk. It's not the behavior that makes the person, but the person that makes the behavior. It's internal to external, not external driving internal.

The truth will set you free, but have you been listening? Faith comes through hearing and hearing by the Word of God. (Romans 10:17) How can you be delivered from the lie if you are making them at home? Have you taken them in and become friends? Surely we wouldn't ask our accuser to make himself at home, so why are we allowing the lies to tuck us into a numb slumber?

Just because this _____ isn't happening, doesn't mean I'm

_____. Just because I am single, does not mean I am unlovable. Don't fill in the blanks with your understanding. Instead, ask God. Let Him fill in the blanks. (Proverbs 3:5–6) Let's stop getting comfortable with lies. Become rooted in truth so that the lie is easily recognizable as a weed that doesn't belong in your garden.

This Too Shall Pass

I'M SORRY TO THOSE WHO were left with moments of short temper, frustration, and pain. Inside was a war I was unwilling to hand over to the Lord. I was a willing participant refusing to know that God has me—that He already won. I wanted to wrestle my demons into submission thinking somehow I had authority apart from God. If I just held it together long enough, all the pain would go away. It would be like it never happened, and suddenly the hellish reality I often find myself in would turn in an instant, but that's delusional.

It did happen, all of it. I'm living breathing proof. It's proven in my muffled shower cries and stares into the distance, breaking away from reality and joining what I conjure up in my mind. It's proven by the distancing no one is sharp enough to grasp as I see myself out of participation. No matter how much I replay memories, they fade. Time slips away, and I'm left with endless yesterdays.

The thief stole all of it under a guise, and I just let it happen. I feel ashamed for having ever loved and pursued what I should have left alone. I feel angry with myself for not calling a news station or fighting more. I slipped right into defeat—a form I knew too well.

I don't want to be here anymore to do this fight. I'm tired. I'm worn, and my heart is heavy. It's burdensome, and it comes down to an intentional effort to yield the burden to God. Will it ever fully go away or is this my portion?

I'd like to say that those words were written years ago, but those feelings were jotted down in September 2023. Only two months later, I wrote what follows. I've tried on His shoes too many times to count, thinking that this time I can do it alone. What a lie. It's okay. Lies come and go. We need only see them out by reminding ourselves of the truth.

Thank you to the things that didn't look like God had touched them. They beg for what my faith is grounded in. Building character is what we call it, but testing faith is its true form.

If we are more than conquerors in Christ, then this too shall pass. According to brain scientist Dr. Jill Bolt Taylor, feelings last for ninety seconds like ocean waves. We can either be overcome by the wave or learn to ride it and let it settle.

Faith without testing is like hope deferred. Deferred means postponed or rejected. Faith tested is true. Faith is hope in what is not yet seen. If we don't have hope in what has yet to come, we have unbelief. We reject the idea that God can do it.

Take the analogy of the man lost at sea. God sends a rescue several times, but the man ends up dying because he had a preconceived idea of what rescue looked like. When a wave comes, we trust that the waters will still again. Be still and know that He is God. If He said it, He will do it, but you must believe it is true. It's easier to let God be God then it is to try on His shoes. This too shall pass. The wave will settle again. Look at the impossible, and speak what is possible by the one who is Waymaker.

Even the Impossible Is Possible

TODAY I RECEIVED A CALL from my sister telling of a woman and her children in a similar predicament as myself, except after the judge who tried my case retired, the adoption hearing for her case was canceled and extended. After hanging up the phone, already irritated by work mishaps, I realized that while I was angry, I was devastated. Don't get me wrong, it is beautiful that she was able to see her children, and I'd never wish what happened to my family on any other, but why couldn't that have been me? Unlike many families plagued with drug addiction or actual abuse and neglect, I was innocent as my children's mother with tainted truths, lies, and slander as my resting place. Where was my miracle? I called my ex-husband; he understands the anger and pain, the uncontrollable traumatic rabbit hole that my mind goes down, long-lost Alice stuck in the "Queen's court." I cried and lashed out memories of sorrow and anger. How could so many get away with what they did?

But then, I recalled the ways God has been good to me in the midst of loss and trial. Had I not lost everything, I would never know God the way I do now. I wouldn't have a close bond with my mom, grandma, and sister. I would've remained in a state of begging for love. My daughters would've missed out on having two God-fearing mothers. Even as I write this, it's not all sunshine and rainbows. It is bittersweet, the kind that leaves a bitter residue but gives short bursts of goodness. I found God in this place.

The "why" no longer matters, but the "what now" is something I am itching to get behind because I am fueled by justice and peace. I want to fight for those who are going through similar court cases, those riddled with opinions and laced with hate, control, and the urge to separate. Let me tell you just how many times I heard the lions whisper reunification was their aim as they blotted out our names. Slander and libel are punishable by law, but not here in small-town America. In small-town America, bitties in a beauty shop can be found around every corner, regardless of how well they knew you as a child.

During my court case, I came upon a book titled *Before We Were Yours*, and the two small blonde girls sitting next to one another on suitcases whispered to me no matter the bookstore, device, or thought I was in. One day, years after the first unction, I picked up the book and read the back. My face melted with tears. I picked up this book for a reason, and the fear started in that moment. *Before We Were Yours* is a fictional depiction of a family stolen off their family's boat and sold by the Tennessee Children's Home Society to a rich family. Irony? I think not. It gets worse. The Tennessee Children's

Home Society made history when Miss Georgia Tann was found out for all her evil dealings. She stole children, bought and sold them to homes, lied, and stretched truths to make a quick buck all while painting herself as their hero. Talk about a Savior Complex. This woman had so much blood on her hands.

A second book was written called *Before and After*. This book marries the real-life stories of the adopted to the other book of fictional depiction. The adoption records were locked up following the 1920s to 1950s scandal. This is NOT a conspiracy theory—it happened. A theory is an idea to explain what happened. A theory is not fact. Unfortunately, we have learned how easy it is to victimize a group of people under a lie and force their hand into believing something by muting or deleting the truth. The second book was a collection of stories told by some of those adopted, long after they were stolen and sold. Many didn't get the chance to reconcile with their parents or siblings. Some as elders met their siblings but everyone else had passed.

Stories like these are some of the roots still lingering beneath our childcare system. Just as injustice does not end with one man or one generation, neither does bitterness, discord, separation, or slander from a wicked system. The culprit? Evil. It lurks everywhere, even in the church. The Bible tells us that even the demons believe. Did I get too heavy on you? Stripped down to its basic form, we take who and what we identify with, the hurts, the anger, the pain, the envy, the evil, and all else (the good stuff too—let's not get too morbid) wherever we go. Systematically, the problem is not the whole entity or all police officers, all judges, or our entire legal system (while it is certainly not built on love, freedom, second chances, or forgiveness), people are the problem. We don't strip who we are the moment we put our work uniform on or when we walk into a church building. No matter how hard one may try to fit the expectations or the atmosphere they are moving into, the roots of who we are seep into the soil we stand on. Think about the honeymoon stage. A new relationship or a new job starts, and all is well. Give it a few weeks or months and the atmosphere changes on a dime. Why? We can only keep our masks on for so long. Sooner or later, we have to come up for air.

From the moment I picked up that book, I knew I was supposed to write my story, but fear held me back until now. What else do I have to lose? What more do I have to gain? The more dependent on God I am, the more I realize that His say-so is the only one I care about. Talk is cheap, and you know what they say about opinions. They're like...I'm sure I don't have to finish that line. God knows my heart, and when I am in line with Him, I couldn't care less about the rest; it's just noise. Tune it out!

Take some time and research the Tennessee Home Society. Research how much it costs to adopt a child or what promotes adoption? I know someone who spent twenty to forty thousand dollars to adopt their daughter. Everyone else, untouched by this corruption, may see that as a worthwhile costly gift. I see something more sinister behind closed doors. When researching adoption costs, the cost varies from twenty to forty-five thousand dollars. Now we know that anything promoted by the need for funding can easily be corrupted. Plenty of good people are in this line of work, and I don't think we throw the baby out with the bath water here, but our family court needs a serious overhaul! Facts are not considered by states not looking at intent. If it happened in your care or someone else's doesn't matter. It happened. Criminal court, on the other hand, has come a long way. There is proof that it was looked into. Facts matter. Family court is disturbing at best.

Trafficking is the buying and selling of a child. If a system of "protection" is driven by funding, then what else would you call the foster care system? The movie *The Sound of Freedom* is only the beginning of whistle-blowing.

Where does God fit into this? It looks pretty bad, right? Yeah, it does, but He is bigger than any evil we can witness, have a hand in, or experience. If Jesus can give His own life and be an example to forgive them, they know not what they do, then so can we. I am frustrated and deeply saddened by the families and children who are lied about and separated and by the torment it has caused, but I do not believe that we fight fire with fire. I believe that we cannot repay sin with sin. We are directed to love our enemies and bless those who curse us. It is the deep-rooted lies that can direct our paths. We become what we believe, and if we believe the lies, we can reproduce the very thing we fear most becoming. I don't hate those who did what they did to my family. I do earnestly forgive them, but I do hate what they did.

We are not our behavior, and this stem we have created has been determined by the accuser—you are this because you did that. Rather, the truth is, you believe this lie and become a thing that looks like the lie. I've always despised one thing about AA meetings as I've had friends and family who've attended. "Hello, my name is and I'm an _____." No, you're not. You are the righteousness of God. You are loved. You were paid for at a high cost to be made one with Him—to look like Him, to be as He is. Where is there room for such a slanderous accusation to rest when you know who you are? It's easy to prey on those who don't know who they are or who they belong to.

How much easier is it to prey on someone in the schoolyard with their head hanging low with no one to protect them? Much easier. Those with a big brother or sister know not to mess with a little sister or brother. When I was in college, a group called Rehab or something like that came to visit. They help women and children who have been sex trafficked escape. I learned that the traffickers target those who walk a certain way. Why? It reveals what they believe. Women and children who walk with their heads low reveal little to no confidence.

Likewise, it was easy to prey on me. I had no idea who I was. I knew I was a good mother, but that's all I knew. I was a wife who had no idea how to love her husband. He silently suffered from PTSD, and I was so caught up in fulfilling my identity as a mother that I didn't see it. Even my identity as a mother wasn't enough. One day, your children move on, they move out and have a family of their own, and if your identity was solely as a parent, you'll find out when they leave. Everything falls apart, and the term *empty nester* applies. This term reveals that our identity was in what is temporary. Yes, you are a mother or a father, but that is not all you are. Yes, you are a husband or a wife, but that is not all you are. When I lost my children and my husband and best friend, I lost me. My identity was not rooted in a strong foundation, so when they were gone, I didn't know who I was.

I have been on a journey of discovering myself for almost seven years now since it all happened. I was always me, but she was buried beneath everything else. There is so much external pressure to be all the things, to be a Pinterest mom or a GI Joe dad without too much "toxic" masculinity. If our identities are formed from the outside in, we will be buried by the weight of it. We must identify from within because what is inside comes out. You can't give something you don't have. What's inside will come out. It doesn't matter what job title you have, who everyone thinks you are, or who you want to be, who you are will be revealed. It will manifest. Listen to what God says about you. Let Him have the final say. The pain of this world is avoidable if we live by a different set of rules or rather no rules, just believing the right things and letting that yield good fruit. If you don't let God in the hidden places, they will come bursting through the doors of your heart. Abandonment. Hate. Pain. Fear. Thy kingdom come, thy will be done on earth as it is in heaven. We need to give those painful things to the Lord. You will cut people on the broken things you have not submitted, even with the best of intentions.

I've dropped the ball as a parent, as a wife, as a friend—in every area of my life. Hurt colored my lens instead of Jesus. How can you give grace you don't believe you have? How can you accept a gift if your hands are full? If you have it all together, what need do you have of God? Just like rose-colored glasses, our perception needs to be yielded to Him and not our own. Our understanding is not His.

So, yes, our world is in desperate need of the Lord, but He shines in the "impossible" and in the barren places. Come and do a new thing. We want Your way. Give us new eyes to perceive as You do. Let us pray for those who need delivered from the lie so that the truth will set them free. Let us start with the man in the mirror.

Generational Curses

Do you know what a curse is? The Hebrew word for *curse* is *Aarar*, meaning to make powerless. The opposite of a curse is a blessing, so what does that make a curse? A word. The vast western church has made this idea of "generational curses" to have some strange power over us beyond what it needs to. If a curse is just a lie, what are the lies that are being passed down in your family?

How do you oppose a lie? With truth. Live different. Show, don't tell. I'm sure we can do some guessing as to the amount of hearts the picketing "Brimstone and Fire" preachers are leading. I remember being at Kent State University, and a group of people handed out these "hell" pamphlets. I threw mine away, appalled at the tactic. Every behavior has a source, a root. If you spend all your time looking at the leaves of a weed and plucking them, what happens beneath the surface? The weed keeps growing and expanding its roots. If Jesus died for all to have life and life abundant, if we are not under the old covenant, if we are told to love our enemies and bless those who curse us, then does the picketer look like Jesus and His way?

Our being the hands and feet of Jesus is what reflects the heart of the Father. It shows what we have faith in. It is easy to spot a phony, someone who doesn't believe in what they're selling. True passion and love, heart change, reflect it. Did you know that there have been studies on which groups of people give more willingly? Who do you suppose it is? It is those who have lost all or have been in "those" shoes before. Those with less tend to give more. That is a sad, harsh reality.

Curses—who gives words power? We do, when we speak them again and AGAIN. Or we play them on repeat in our minds. What we believe of ourselves is manifest in the way we live our lives. Do we love the people? Are we reaching out to the broken, the needy, those who don't know the love of God or are we stuck behind the walls of our church? Last I checked, we are the church, and that means we take the Lord everywhere with us. It's important to be plugged into the body, but if we are only plugged in to leave the rest of the week limp, we have missed the point. We are called to go and make disciples. This doesn't mean to raise hell and tell everyone what they are doing wrong. Did Jesus hold up picket signs and scream and condemn? Nope. In fact, He washed feet. He healed. He set free people who were believing lies about themselves. Pick up your mat and follow Me!

Words have POWER. Don't give power to those words that don't line up with what the Lord says about you. You don't need anyone's approval but His. These "generational curses" are only the lies that your family passes down. Lay hold of the lies in your own garden (mind) and find the root. Let the Lord show you the root and the truth. The truth will set you free. You need only believe. Believe in His words, not the curses (lies). When it comes to the family, discover the root, apply the truth, and live it. That's it. Set the example. When the impossible is made possible in your life because you are submitted to the Lord, all will see His hand in it and ask how.

Feed your mind with the truth, uproot the lies, and walk out what you believe.

Sealed by the Blood

GOD REVEALS TO REDEEM. He asks you to take a leap, knowing He will catch you. It may not look like you are winning or it may look like a giant Goliath is in the way, but it must bow at the name of Jesus. We partner with God by listening to that thing He calls us to obey. Do it scared. Take the leap. He honors obedience. That is true faith, behaving like you believe Him. I won't be left disappointed, because I am partnering with Him, obeying what He has asked, and believing that the promise sealed by the blood tells me He will never let His kids down.

What are you scared of? If He told you to do it, He will meet you there in the waiting for the very thing He is asking you to prepare for. He has authority over all things. Don't make your Goliath bigger than God. If they stand in the way of the promise, they've got to move. This promise is not just about you. It's about setting a standard. No man or lie can stand in the way of the blood of the Lamb. Your promise has been sealed. It just takes you believing and meeting Him there. Act like you believe Him.

Consider the covenant made with Abraham, the promise God gave to him and his descendants. In Genesis 17, the covenant promise God gave to Abraham starts with the foundation of "I am Almighty God; walk before Me and be blameless and I will make My covenant between me and you, and will multiply you exceedingly."

Reading on, and after Abram fell to His face, God said, "As for Me, behold, My covenant is with you, and you shall be a father of many nations." God changes Abram's name to Abraham meaning "Father of many nations." A name represents a new identity and that identity was fashioned in Abraham's purpose. This covenant was given to Abraham and his descendants. If you track the lineage of Abraham, you'll find that Jesus was a part of it. Jesus was the Father and is the Father of many nations. God was arranging a bigger purpose, a gift. While establishing this covenant, God spoke as if Abraham already had many descendants, but his wife, Sarah, was barren. Sarah was ninety and he ninety-nine—talk about "impossible" odds. The odds are in your favor just as they were in this situation.

Fast forward and let's visit the blood covenant made by God through Himself in the form of man, the Son of God, Jesus. Before Jesus shed His blood for all, religious practices held the people to stipulations of blood covering. Lambs and other animals were sacrificed for the atonement of sin. Visiting Hebrews 9, we see that Jesus's blood replaced the old covenant with a new covenant. "...how much more shall the blood of Christ, who through the eternal Spirit offered Himself without spot to God, cleanse your conscience from dead works to serve the living God?" (Hebrews 9:14)

Blood was the currency needed in the old covenant and with the new covenant; however, Jesus was without spot, fully self-sacrificed to tear the veil between us and God by acting as the mediator.

The word *conscience* is taken from the Greek word *suneidesis* which can be broken down into two parts: "to know" and "with." The veil being torn is having perfect union with our Father because of what was done through Jesus. Now, this connection allows Him and ourselves to partner together to cleanse our conscience and unveil our ignorance of His understanding. We know that we can cast "down arguments and every high thing that exalts itself against the knowledge of God, bringing every thought into captivity to the obedience of Christ." (2 Corinthians 10:5)

We ask ourselves, what does God say about this matter. When the thought arises that opposes the "knowledge of God," we do not pull out a switchblade on our thoughts. We feed ourselves the truth.

Let's look at the who, what, when, where, and why of this text in Matthew when Satan tempted Jesus by saying, "If You are the Son of God, command this stone to become bread." (Luke 4:3)

This was following an act of obedience, seeking out intimate time with the Father during a forty-day fast. Jesus responded with truth saying, "It is written, 'Man shall not live by bread alone, but by every word of God.'" (Luke 4:4)

His weapon was using his tongue to speak the Word. The Word of God is actually broken into two parts: *rhema* meaning "utterance" or "things said" and *Logos* or "the written word." The word and the tongue are both compared to a weapon. "And He has made My mouth like a sharp sword..." (Isaiah 49:2)

The Word of God is also called "living and powerful, and sharper than any two-edged sword, piercing even to the division of soul and spirit, and of joints and marrow, and is a discerner of the thoughts and intents of the heart." (Hebrews 4:12)

Pair our mouthpiece with the Word of God and we've got one heck of an AK-47—spiritually, that is! This is when we come into agreement with the promise of God. The testimony of Christ is having been dead, He was raised again, defeating death. Testimony is from the Hebrew word *aydooth* meaning "to do with the same power and authority." He wants to do it for you too! Take that lie that you are counted. It's not for you. Cut it down with the sword of your mouth declaring the sword of truth!

His bloodshed was royal. The price paid for you to live in truth was expensive, not in vain. Below, write the lies you've known, and renew your mind with what God says!

Lies

_____

_____

_____

_____

_____

_____

_____

_____

Scripture Truth

_____

_____

_____

_____

_____

_____

_____

_____

_____

_____

_____

_____

_____

_____

_____

_____

_____

Ending

I STAND FOR THOSE WHO believed the lie that they didn't have a seat at the table. He uses the least of these, the foolish to counsel the wise. Take a seat. Eat and be made well.

This may be my story, but it's not about me. A life laid down serves others. It doesn't matter who believes me and who doesn't. It doesn't matter whether I am liked or not. What outlasts the noise, the applause, and the approval is God's approval. It's His pride in His child for extending a hand to those who are overlooked. If one person puts down the vice, looks to the Father, or relinquishes the grip on a steel trigger, I've done my job. I'd rather obey God and upset every person in the room than find applause and noise at the gain of a Grinch-sized heart. God has parted the waters so that we might walk through apart from what we were born into, apart from the pain, and ready to take the risk and take His hand.

Whatever your present moment looks like, remember what He has done for David, Job, Sarah, Abraham, and all of the other names who bear life and strength to our bones—hope to our spirit. "Your testimonies I have taken as a heritage forever." (Psalm 119:111)

It is the reminder of testimony, stories of conquering, and grit that cause our feet to run with endurance, knowing full well that our Father will do for us as He has done before with the "same power and authority." Heritage is your tangible promise, inheritance, land. It is what belongs to you naturally—without earning, striving, or pleading for governance. It is yours because of who your Father is.

As with any relationship, you must spend uninterrupted, genuine time with someone to grow a relationship with them. If you want to believe in what He can do for you and through you, get to know Him. When you get to know someone, truly, you have confidence in what they say. You respect their words because you know their heart and can deduce intention. So, regardless of the Goliath in your life, run to your Papa. He is waiting for you just like the prodigal son, never harboring any shame or anger and long awaiting his return home.

This is your home, and you'll never find the grieved for peace you long for outside of it. The thing about your Goliath is that God made it. Whether it is a judge, an attorney, a neighbor, or a family member, God breathed life into their bones. Not only is He bigger than any problem we face, but He is stronger and wiser than the things of this world. We are limited in our capacity to see the whole picture, but God. BUT GOD! He is infinite in all of His ways, never lacking nor defined by man—no matter what their temporary man-given authority. You need not flap your wings and exert your strength. Soar on His promises, allowing Him to be your defense. He knows the hearts and minds of those around you, including yourself, better than you can know you or hope to fill in the blanks of another. He can and He will do it for you! The Bible is the most controversial book in any land because of truth. Truth will set the captives free. Crack it open and discover the love your Father has for you and all He created you to be.

Going to church, reading testimonials, and having fellowship are all good things, but they cannot replace intimate time with the Father. "So then faith comes by hearing, and hearing by the Word of God." (Romans 10:17)

Faith is grown by hearing the truth from His Word. Our brains are wired to believe in what we hear repetitively. Have you ever considered the marketing tactics of social media? If you see it enough and hear it enough, you are soon pushing that order button. Have my money—have all of it. Seek and you shall find. Knock and the door will be opened to you. (Matthew 7:7) "You will seek Me and find Me, when you search for Me with all your heart." (Jeremiah 29:13)

Seek. Knock. Ask. Be still and know. He is God and we are not. Be encouraged that you are not forgotten. You are the branch and He the vine, one. Connected.

Always remember, BUT GOD! Everyone loves a good underdog story—get up and keep swinging, Rocky!

Don't you know, flowers grow in the rain.

Take Action

Without application, do you really believe it? Here are a few exercises you can do by yourself or with loved ones to expose the lies and dismantle them.

1. Go to your mirror and unveil the lies. What does your past say? Others? What doesn't line up with what God says? Write with dry erase marker. Now cross it out and replace it with what God says. You could even do this with a group of spirit-filled women or at a Bible study. Use a floor-length mirror, bathroom mirror, or handheld dollar store mirror. Each person sits looking in the mirror while friends speak the truth of who they see and write the words accordingly on their reflection.

2. A game with friends, kids, or children. You can do this several ways. You can pin the lie to a cross on a piece of paper, write the lie on paper and set it on fire, or write lies on a dollar store plate and break them. The last one was my fourteen-year-old sister's idea—we did that!

3. You can take inventory personally in a bullet journal through lists and creativity or paint the lies and the truth. Whatever the means, get honest about the lies you are feeding on and taste His goodness and what He says instead.

About the Author

Christine Matics is a small town girl with big-hearted dreams, dirty feet, and a thrill for the buzz of nature. Her passion is to love people right where they are, reviving the art of evangelism. She spends her days with her son, gardening, traveling, and making spiritual connections. She is a writer, worshipper, watercolor painter, and all things DIY fanatic. Light Up the Dark: An Interactive Memoir is her first book of many as she has several children's books in the works for future release.